Glimpses of Heaven from
Great Literary Classics

. . . .

JOURNEY
TO THE
CELESTIAL
CITY

. . . .

WAYNE MARTINDALE, PH.D.
EDITOR

MOODY PRESS
CHICAGO

© 1995
WAYNE MARTINDALE

Scripture quotations marked (NASB) are taken from the *New American Standard Bible.*

Scripture quotations marked (NIV) are taken from the *Holy Bible: New International Version*®. NIV®.

Scripture quotations marked (RSV) are taken from the *Revised Standard Version.*

Scripture quotations marked (NRSV) are taken from the *New Revised Standard Version.*

Scripture quotations marked (KJV) are taken from the *King James Version.*

The use of selected references from various versions of the Bible in this publication does not necessarily imply publisher endorsement of the versions in their entirety.

ISBN: 0-8024-4347-8

1 3 5 7 9 10 8 6 4 2

Printed in the United States of America

For my daughter
Heather Martindale
who has brightened my journey

CONTENTS

CONTRIBUTORS

E. Beatrice Batson, Ph.D., Vanderbilt University, chair of the English department at Wheaton College, Wheaton, Illinois, from 1975–88, now serves as coordinator of the Shakespeare Collection at the College. She has authored several books, including a literary study of John Bunyan's *The Pilgrim's Progress* written for the schools of England and is editor of two recent volumes on Shakespeare: *The Christian Dimension of Shakespearean Drama* and *Shakespeare and the Christian Tradition*.

Rolland Hein, Ph.D., Purdue University, Clyde S. Kilby Professor of English at Wheaton College, Wheaton, Illinois, is an internationally known MacDonald scholar. His books on MacDonald include several editions of his works, a critical assessment called *The Harmony Within: The Spiritual Vision of George MacDonald*, and the most authoritative biography on the author to date, *George MacDonald: Victorian Mythmaker*.

Wayne Martindale, Ph.D., University of California, Riverside, is associate professor of English at Wheaton College, Wheaton, Illinois. He has lectured and written several articles on C. S. Lewis and is coeditor of *The Quotable Lewis*.

Barbara Reynolds, Ph.D., University of London, a scholar of international renown, was lecturer in Italian for twenty-two years at Cambridge University. She is editor of the *Cambridge Italian Dictionary* and a translator of Dante, including a portion of *The Divine Comedy* left unfinished at the death of her friend Dorothy L. Sayers. Among her many books and articles is *The Passionate Intellect: Dorothy L. Sayers' Encounter with Dante.*

Daniel E. Ritchie, Ph.D., Rutgers University, is associate professor of English at Bethel College, St. Paul, Minnesota, where he teaches eighteenth-century literature. He has edited two books on Edmund Burke and has written on Burke, Johnson, Pope, and Matthew Arnold. He has a forthcoming book (Eerdmans, 1996) on Milton, Swift, Pope, Johnson, and Burke that responds to recent ideological criticism with a biblical poetics.

Leland Ryken, Ph.D., University of Oregon, has authored a score of books on various aspects of Christianity and literature, including *Milton and Scriptural Tradition: The Bible into Poetry* and *Realms of Gold: The Classics in Christian Perspective.* He is professor of English and chair of the English department at Wheaton College, Wheaton, Illinois.

Manfred Siebald, Ph.D., University of Marburg, is professor of American literature at Johannes Gutenberg University in Mainz, Germany. His publications include essays on Herman Melville and an intellectual biography of Dorothy Sayers, as well as a recently completed ten-year study on the theme of the prodigal son in literature. He is also a noted Christian singer-songwriter, whose performances and recordings are well known throughout Europe.

Gene Edward Veith, Jr., Ph.D., University of Kansas, is associate professor of English and dean of the College of Arts and Sciences at Concordia University, Milwaukee, Wisconsin. He is the author of many books, including *Loving God with All Your Mind; State of the Arts: From Bezalel to Mapplethorpe;* and *Reading Between the Lines: A Christian Guide to Literature.*

ACKNOWLEDGMENTS

I happily acknowledge a lifelong debt to Dr. George Musacchio, who awakened my interest in literature generally and to C. S. Lewis particularly. Through classes and in-office talks, through trips to Modern Language Association conventions and C. S. Lewis Society meetings, he nurtured my late-blooming love of learning, books, and great literature. He is still my mentor and model, and, gratefully, my friend.

I am also daily challenged and encouraged by gifted colleagues in the English department at Wheaton. They are both directly and indirectly responsible for this book. First, three of them have contributed chapters: Beatrice Batson, who hired me at Wheaton and gave leadership to the English department for so many years; Lee Ryken, present chair and unfailing encourager; and Rolland Hein, Kilby Chair and masterful teacher of what we call "modern myth."

Without Beatrice Batson, I would never have gotten to know Barbara Reynolds, who has often regaled both faculty and students with wit and wisdom both at Wheaton and in England on our summer treks with students. Dr. Batson also brought Ed Veith into our departmental orbit as visiting professor in my early days at the college. He has stimulated me to good works through nearly fifteen years, and Thanksgiving with the Veith family is now a firmly entrenched Martindale family tradition.

Without Alan Jacobs I would never have met Manfred Siebald and family. Manfred's scholarship and Christian spirit have given me a new understanding of what it means to be a disciple of Christ in the academy. To my other colleagues, Jill Baumgaertner, Sharon Coolidge, Jeff Davis, Sarah Fodor, Paul Fromer, Kent Gramm, Gail Kienitz, Roger Ludin, and secretary Angie Aubrey, thank you for creating an environment where work and ministry are a stimulating challenge, a joy, and a reward.

It must be gratefully acknowledged that the book would not have happened without Jim Bell, editorial director at Moody Press. The book was his idea, and I'm thankful that he entrusted me with the execution of the project. His breadth, professionalism, and collegiality have made him a joy to work with.

Finally, besides making life rich and joyful, my wife, Vaneta, and daughter, Heather, read the manuscript and made, as always, valuable suggestions and corrections.

This book is a traveler's guide for the heavenward bound. Its premise is a biblical one. Like Abraham, "by faith" we are living in this world as aliens and are "looking for the city which has foundations, whose architect and builder is God" (Hebrews 11:8–10 NASB). As Paul reminds us, "our citizenship is in heaven" (Philippians 3:20 NASB).

With these thoughts, our minds rush to several questions: What is the city of our citizenship like? What relevance does my earthly journey have to my heavenly home? If I am a citizen of heaven and an alien in my earthly journey, how am I to live now? Does the way I live now have a bearing on how I will live in eternity? Where can I find guides to help me through this worldly maze?

Good answers and good guides are hard to find. Our best source, as always, is the Bible. And in every age, the Holy Spirit has given the church gifted people to aid in making the timeless Word relevant to the time and culture of their generation. Like the Bible itself, the best of these have elements that transcend their historical moment.

THE NEED FOR LITERATURE
ON JOURNEYING TO HEAVEN

It should not be surprising that some of the best help in understanding heaven and our heavenward journey comes from Christian literary classics. Just as Jesus taught mainly with stories, He has gifted others to teach with stories. Judging from Jesus' persistent use of parables, it seems clear that what "the kingdom of heaven is like" comes across best in story form. Abstractions and "scientific" descriptions of what "eye has not seen and ear has not heard" would inevitably be misleading. It's safer to use fiction, which will not be taken for literal truth, but which, like Jesus' stories, can tell the truth indirectly yet powerfully.

For example, Dante's portrait of heaven is not likely to be mistaken as a physical place. He himself insists that it is only an attempt to describe the indescribable and make clear to limited human faculties what may be known by the power of suggestion. By means of characters, events, and symbols, we come to understand ideas like free will, reward and punishment, the nature of love, the psychology of temptation, the inexhaustible glory and complexity of God. We come to feel as well as know that our own good is served in serving Him, that we are more fully ourselves in Christ.

Each of the literary classics presented here involves journeys. The journey is the oldest archetype or pattern in literature, going back to the Old Testament journey of the Israelites under Moses and to the ancient Greek epics as well. Typically, the journey and its challenges bring out the character of the hero and symbolize the spiritual, moral, and ethical development of the hero and the hero's culture. It is a powerful organizing device, which appeals to readers of every generation.

Narratives appeal to our imagination in a way that the abstractions of theology do not. Stories give us an experience and make us feel. Fear, longing, revulsion, exultation: these and more are all there. Stories make us wise beyond our lived experience, and they motivate us. Here is value and benefit, indeed. The chief reason for investing the time to understand and value this deeply Christian literature is that it reawakens our longing for Home and strengthens our hearts, minds, and souls for the rigors of the journey while preparing us for the joys along the way: those foretastes of heaven vouchsafed to us even now.

Each of the narratives in this volume reminds us that the journey is ultimately to God and that Christ is the way. If redemption is the first step, attaining Christlikeness is the path we travel, and the Celestial City (heaven) is at once the end and beginning of the journey. Chronicling the great variety of obstacles from within and without and the heroic possibilities for overcoming them in the grace and sovereignty of God is the stories' reason for being.

WHAT YOU WILL FIND IN THIS BOOK

This book presents the vision of heaven and the related sense of pilgrimage as conceived by a few of the world's greatest writers. In each case, the aim is to help the reader more profoundly envision heaven and to lend assistance in the earthly journey that leads there. Eight literary figures are the subject of this study: Augustine, Dante, Bunyan, Milton, Defoe, Stowe, MacDonald, and Lewis. We focus on one key work by each author, with the exception of two for MacDonald.

Each chapter includes a short bibliography of selected readings at the end. The bibliographies include important editions readily available and the most useful commentary for the nonspecialist.

Essays should be accessible to those who have never read a given writer but should be of interest to those who have read the works but could use help in focusing on the theme of heaven and pilgrimage. We have tried to make the essays interesting to the general reader, yet substantive and authoritative. Each author is a recognized authority on his or her assigned author. Our intentions are:

— to help readers better understand heaven and live as citizens of that kingdom;
— to develop in readers a desire to read the great mind-expanding, spirit-awakening literature on heaven;
— to provide a framework for reading the originals with greater understanding;
— to help make the works more accessible to the general reader.

These are some of the questions we asked about the works:

— What is the author's view of heaven?
— How is the character of the journey shaped by this vision?
— How are the characters being suited for heaven?
— To what extent are the characters experiencing heaven now?
— What are the main impediments to a successful pilgrimage as envisioned by the writer?

— How are these overcome?

— What does the writer have to say about spiritual warfare, drawing apart from and/or engaging the world, and seeking heavenly things?

— What is unique in the way the pilgrimage or search is conducted or presented?

— How does the author connect with universal needs, desires, and questions?

Since heaven is beyond our experience, and Scripture asserts that we can't even imagine its splendor, how do writers meet the challenge of presenting it? The opening chapter is a short discussion by Leland Ryken on the techniques writers typically use to talk about heaven. This chapter will be a useful beginning point even if readers wish to skip around in what follows.

After the chapter on methodology, the organization is chronological, spanning seventeen centuries. The genres (literary types) range from autobiography to epic poem to novel to fantasy, and include both poetry and fiction. The works discussed have a geographical spread from North Africa to Europe to North America. While all of the commentators are evangelicals (though from a variety of denominations), the primary literature is written by authors of varied theological persuasion. This diversity has the benefits of (1) giving us many perspectives on a subject that stretches even the best imaginations, (2) suggesting the universality of the subject's appeal, and (3) showing that writers from wide-ranging backgrounds all share a core of biblical truth—what C.S. Lewis called "mere Christianity."

For all of their diversity, the primary authors have in common several elements besides the foundational "mere Christianity," that is, firm belief that the central issue is salvation in Christ. All the works studied in this book are classics: they have played key roles in shaping the literature, the thought, and the culture of many nations. The enduring popularity of the works attests to the strength and importance of each. Each of the pieces also deals with the theme of choice and says in its own way, "Choose this day whom you will serve" (Joshua 24:15 RSV).

Every generation since their writing has found that each of these Christian classics is relevant for our journey to heaven. Just a little help is all that is often needed to open up the treasure coined in another country at another time.

Ed Veith's lead piece on Augustine beautifully illustrates how the more things change, the more they remain the same. From Augustine's bondage to hedonism to his analysis of culture in moral crisis, we see both ourselves and national problems illuminated. Augustine lived at a time when Rome was under siege and Christianity was even being blamed for national problems. How did "the greatest intellect of the early church" respond? How should citizens of heaven handle their earthly citizenship? How does seeing the bigger picture bring personal relationships into focus? In many ways, Augustine was a thoroughgoing product of secular culture: he had it made politically; his worldview was self-centered and power-conscious. But when he converted as an adult, he became a leading critic of secular culture and an advocate of Christian alternatives.

Dante knew political and personal turmoil too. No ivory-tower visions of heaven from him. He lived through exile and civil war. Dante knew human evil "up close and personal," as shown by his inclusion of so many historical figures in the poem. It was his profound understanding of sin that confirmed for him the necessity of hell for those who chose sin. His keener understanding of sin is the backdrop for his jubilation over redemption and inexpressible joy of heaven.

How good is Dante on heaven? C. S. Lewis, after reading *Paradiso* (Paradise or Heaven), wrote to his lifelong friend Arthur Greeves that Dante "opened a new world to me" (*Letters to Greeves* 325). In Lewis's view, "Dante remains a strong candidate for the supreme poetical honours of the world" (*Selected Literary Essays* 204). Not everyone would see what Lewis saw (nor did he see it all the first time through). Clearly, the most difficult piece to read is Dante's *Divine Comedy* (but Barbara Reynold's chapter on this work is not difficult to read). Nothing which attempts to cover earthly history plus heaven and hell, using the whole known universe as a setting, is going to be a snap. But as Lewis says, "There is so much besides poetry in Dante that anyone but a fool can enjoy him in some way or other" (*Studies in Medieval* 76).

Like Dante, Milton was in the thick of civil war. He was the modern American equivalent of secretary of state to Oliver Cromwell, who was for over a decade the most powerful political figure in England. When Cromwell's government fell, Milton had to stay on the move and lie low for a time to avoid arrest. He knew the utopian hope for an earthly "City of God" and the disillusionment of those who place their hope in it. As if these trials were not enough, Milton was stricken with blindness in his prime. But in his loss of sight, Milton prayed for spiritual insight. God granted the request, and *Paradise Lost* is part of the evidence. The poem is, as Lee Ryken says, "the story of all things." Ryken masterfully guides the reader through Milton's inspired epic vision of the human journey from the loss of .Paradise through sin to redemption by Christ and Paradise regained, opening up the riches of Milton's glimpse of the Celestial City.

From Dante and Milton, whose understanding of human nature is keen but whose reach is so far beyond our usual grasp of the heavenly, we come to Bunyan and Defoe, two writers who focus intensely on everyday experience. They teach us how to live in contentment amidst earthly woe and how every act is sacred—that is, how we may "do all to the glory of God" (1 Corinthians 10:31 KJV).

Everyone at least knows *about* John Bunyan's *The Pilgrim's Progress*. This work of the late seventeenth century has become part of the Christian heritage of every generation to follow. Many will even know that Bunyan wrote this powerful allegory while in prison for his faith. God consoles those who suffer for His name with the liveliest hope of heaven. Beatrice Batson teaches us how to understand Christian's allegorical journey from the City of Destruction to the Celestial City as emblematic of our own journey. He is every man and every woman in his despair without Christ, in hope through redemption, in overcoming great obstacles, and in gaining glory at last.

Most, perhaps from children's books, would recognize the name of Defoe's famous character, Robinson Crusoe, and would probably know that he spent a long time alone on an island before meeting his man Friday. But not many have read the whole book in its original. *Robinson Crusoe* is a profoundly Christian book. As Dan Ritchie shows, the story of Crusoe engages numerous stories of Scripture, from his prodigal and wandering youth to his island conversion and missionary zeal. It is, on the narrative level, the most earthbound of the books discussed in this volume. But Ritchie shows how heaven comes to earth in the life of this character.

Another book born out of civil war is Harriet Beecher Stowe's *Uncle Tom's Cabin*. Uncle Tom is a Christian martyr who goes "walking through fire and singing of heaven." In this chapter, Manfred Siebald examines the music of *Uncle Tom's Cabin*, especially the hymns, which give a unique perspective on the characters' understanding of heaven. It is the hope of heaven that sustains the community of slaves, that enables the characters to cross racial lines, that enables the victims to return good for evil and love their persecutors. This is what motivates social reform while giving personal hope. Siebald poses the question we wish to ask: "If *Uncle Tom's Cabin* is so otherworldly, what explains the profound social and political impact that the novel had?" This extraordinary chapter explains why the heavenly vision is central to its earthly impact.

The last two essays return to writers from Great Britain whom Americans have adopted with almost unparalleled enthusiasm: the Scottish preacher George MacDonald and the Irish/English scholar C. S. Lewis. Lewis said that reading MacDonald as a teenager "baptized" his imagination. Rolland Hein's engaging chapter on MacDonald's two masterpieces, *Phantastes* and *Lilith*, show why. The character Anodos in *Phantastes*, on his journey to Faerie (heaven), struggles with everything from sensuality to fear. He must finally despair of finding personal solutions and die to himself to find himself in Christ. But this is abstraction; *Phantastes* is a mind-expanding adventure story. In *Lilith*, we learn the great potential we have to unmake ourselves in evil or find spiritual wholeness in the "moral splendor" of God.

Lewis enthusiastically acknowledges his profound imaginative and spiritual debt to MacDonald. While MacDonald's works "baptized" Lewis's imagination, Lewis's *The Great Divorce* baptized mine. His story of a journey from hell to heaven captured me as a teenager and has never let me go. In short, I fell in love with heaven. That's the hope and prayer of each author, of the original works and of these commentaries. If after reading this book you love heaven more and are helped on the journey to the Celestial City, our labors will be fully rewarded and our prayers answered.

Scripture teaches, and I believe, that one day this present heaven and earth will pass away—dissolve, as I imagine, from the center of every atom, as every nucleus lets go of every proton, and every electron spins out of orbit, and the universe vanishes like a dream. And Christ the Creator will create a new heaven and a new earth. Then we will see that the spiritual is the true reality, the undeniable fact, more substantial and more durable than the seat you now sit in or ground you stand on.

Until that day, we must grope as best we can for glimpses of the Celestial City and apprehend for the most part by faith. Books written by people with various gifts from the Holy Spirit can help us on the path. They can brace us, as they have generations past, for both the joys and perils along the journey. The chapters that follow are stepping stones that will, for the faithful pilgrim, broaden into the streets of gold.

WORKS CITED

Lewis, C. S. *The Letters of C. S. Lewis to Arthur Greeves (1914–1963).* Edited by Walter Hooper. New York: Collier/Macmillan, 1986.

————. *Selected Literary Essays.* Edited by Walter Hooper. Cambridge: Cambridge Univ. Press, 1979.

————. *Studies in Medieval and Renaissance Literature.* Edited by Walter Hooper. Cambridge: Cambridge Univ. Press, 1966.

THE RHETORIC OF TRANSCENDENCE

BY LELAND RYKEN

To portray heaven as literary authors do requires more than a set of *ideas* about heaven. It also requires a *rhetoric* of transcendence—a repertoire of images, techniques, and formulas. Knowing what these descriptive techniques are will help us to know what to look for in descriptions of heaven and to be more receptive to the effects of those visions. We should remember that in the literature of pilgrimage the journey is not the point; arrival in heaven is.

Writers who portray heaven have seven basic techniques at their disposal. All of their extended descriptions are variations on these seven techniques.

CONTRAST

One of the rhetorical patterns by which writers portray heaven is contrast. Heaven is "other" than what we ordinarily experience, a distinction made explicit in the familiar designation "otherworldly." Of course the contrasts in these heavenly visions build upon familiar realities in *this* world, in effect mingling the familiar and unfamiliar to evoke a picture of something different from ordinary reality.

A simple example from Revelation 21 is references to a "new heaven," a "new earth," and "new Jerusalem." We have *our* versions of heaven, earth, and Jerusalem, but the adjective *new* signals that the heavenly version of them is different. In the same chapter we read that "the city has no need of sun or moon to shine upon it, for the glory of God is its light" (Revelation 21:23 RSV). This is obviously quite a different world from the one we inhabit. In the first extended heavenly scene that we encounter in Milton's *Paradise Lost,* we read about "celestial roses" and "Elysian flowers," with the adjectives alerting us that these objects are somehow different from their counterparts on earth.

One of the formulas by which writers create a sense of contrast between the earthly and heavenly is the comparative formula. Heaven is higher or brighter or better or more permanent than earth. Milton's Satan, for example, finds the light of heaven "beyond expression bright, / Compared with aught on earth" (*Paradise Lost,* 5.361–62). In Milton's poem heaven is not simply bright but "brightest" (5.644), inhabited by "spirits of purest light" (6.660). The beauty that Dante the pilgrim perceives in heaven "transcends . . . all measure of ours," while the light of Bunyan's Celestial City is so much brighter than earthly light that pilgrims approaching it can view it only "through an instrument made for that purpose."

Another contrast, used by virtually all writers who give us extended descriptions of heaven, is based on what past ages called enameled imagery—imagery combining brilliance of light and hardness of texture, with jewels topping the list. In the heavenly visions in the book of Revelation, for example, we read about a sea of glass, a river bright as crystal, and a city that is "pure gold, clear as glass" (21:18 RSV). What are we to make of this imagery that appears with such consistency in visions of heaven? The best explanation is that it exists to evoke a world of superior value, splendor, and permanence than that found our vegetative cyclic world.

By a variety of specific words and formulas, then, writers of the Celestial City convince us that heaven is different from our world. The very scenes and creatures that they describe, as well as the God who fills heaven, make us continuously aware as we read that heaven is a contrast to earthly reality. When Bunyan's Christian sees two "Shining Ones" coming

toward him, we do not need a tour guide to tell us that they are not our
next-door neighbors.

NEGATION

There have traditionally been two approaches to transcendence—the
way of affirmation of images and the way of negation. The latter designation means simply that God and heaven are defined as the absence of
human or earthly reality. For example, we speak of God as infinite (not
finite) and heaven as being endless (without end).

Often the negation is expressed in such a way as to name the thing
that is absent from heaven. In Revelation 21:4 we read that in heaven
"death shall be no more, neither shall there be mourning nor crying nor
pain any more, for the former things have passed away" (RSV). As Bunyan's Christian receives preliminary instruction about his coming life in
heaven, he is told, "There you shall not see again such things as you saw
when you were in the lower region upon the earth, to wit, sorrow, sick-
ness, affliction, and death."

A specific formula of negation that writers through the centuries have
used is the inexpressibility motif, consisting of protestations by the writer
or a character in the story that heaven is beyond human ability to describe
or comprehend. For example, the angels in Milton's heaven praise God's
"goodness beyond thought," and the angels themselves stand "in orbs of
circuit inexpressible." The Shining Ones tell Bunyan's pilgrim regarding
heaven "that the beauty and glory of it are inexpressible." As the pilgrim
Dante nears the final vision of God in heaven, he writes, "From then on
my vision was greater / than our speech, which fails at such a sight."

Beyond these explicit negations, we are simply aware of how simpli-
fied life in heaven is compared to the complex roles and activities that
make up our earthly lives. Citizens of heaven are chiefly worshipers.
Heavenly ritual consists mainly of worship and praise. The literature of
pilgrimage lavishes its attention on the journey to heaven and then
becomes largely silent when the pilgrim finally arrives there, leaving us
with the impression that what goes on there is beyond finite human
understanding. Unless we realize that the technique being used is one of
negation in which the absence of activity signals not poverty but a richness beyond our understanding, we can scarcely avoid sympathizing with
people who try to render the Christian hope of heaven ridiculous by say-

ing that *they* do not want to spend eternity playing harps. The question of what we will do in heaven for eternity remains a mystery to those who have not yet been translated, and reticence is the best way of preserving the mystery.

ANALOGY

The way of negation has always been balanced by the way of affirmation as a means of portraying the transcendent. Using earthly images to portray God and heaven presupposes the principle of analogy between earth and heaven. After all, earthly language and experience are the only materials we have to portray the "other" world.

In earlier centuries the theological doctrine that provided a rationale for portraying heavenly reality in earthly terms was the doctrine of accommodation. The doctrine of accommodation asserts that in the Bible, God, who is spiritual, has accommodated Himself to human understanding by portraying Himself and heavenly reality in humanly understandable images. John Calvin theorized that God is portrayed in physical images in the Bible "to exhibit to us the appearance of spiritual and heavenly things, in a kind of earthly way" (131). Milton made the doctrine of accommodation the principle underlying his extended vision of heaven in *Paradise Lost*. In that poem, as the angel Raphael prepares to tell Adam about the war in heaven, he claims that he will "[liken] spiritual to corporal forms / As may express them best" (5.573–74). He concludes the account with a comment about "measuring things in heaven by things on earth" (6.893).

This principle of analogy is evident in virtually any description of heaven that we might read. Heaven is regularly pictured as a city with gates and streets, for example. In Jesus' evocative version, it is a great "house [with] many rooms" (John 14:2 RSV). Heaven has also been regularly pictured as a kingly court, replete with thrones, crowns, and courtly attendants. Musical harmony has likewise been prevalent, again establishing a link between life in heaven and life on earth.

Writers who portray heaven at any length give it a landscape. It is common to picture it as standing on a hill, mountain, or elevated place. Balancing the urban aspects of heaven are pastoral ones. In the last chapter of the Bible, heaven has a river with trees on both sides of it. Milton's heaven has an abundance of geographical analogies to earthly experience, as we read about hills, fields, trees, and woods. The physical image that dominates virtually all visions of heaven is light.

As for the angels and saints who inhabit heaven, they are recognizable to us. They have bodies, no matter how different they might be from earthly bodies. They have a social structure and hierarchy. They do things together the way people do in earthly communities.

In short, descriptions of heaven are a mingling of the familiar and unfamiliar. The principle of analogy allows writers to include the familiar images of our own experience. Theorists of religious language rightly remind us that we have no otherworldly or supernatural language by which to portray the transcendent; we have only human language and experience.

Analogy like this is metaphoric. At some level the physical image asserts something that is really true of heaven. If heaven is portrayed as a city, the physical image implies the qualities of unity and community that heaven really possesses. Light is both literal and a metaphor of splendor and illumination. Jesus could compare heaven to a stately house with many mansions because there really are connections between a house and heaven—connections like refuge, rest, and living close together.

SYMBOLISM

As we move along the continuum of imagery used to portray heaven, we move away from literal analogy toward symbolism. A symbol is an image that stands for something else. A flag, for example, symbolizes a nation but is in no sense a literal picture of it. White symbolizes purity, but purity is not literally a color.

Symbolism takes greater liberties than analogy does with the physical images used to portray heaven. In analogy, we give a degree of literal belief to the physical image, even if we entertain the possibility that the physical image is not true of heaven in exactly the ordinary way. It seems inevitable, for example, that heaven does really possess some of the qualities of a city and house, whereas the pearly gates and golden streets are probably symbolic.

The use of symbolism to portray heaven begins in the Bible. Topping the list is the book of Revelation, where glorified believers are pictured as symbolically receiving such things as the morning star (2:28), a white stone with a secret name written on it (2:17), and water from a fountain of life (21:6).

Similar symbolism is used to portray the citizens who inhabit heaven. Daniel's prophecy pictures them as shining "like the stars for ever and ever" (12:3 NIV), a symbol of their glory but not a literal picture of what they are. Revelation 14:4 claims that the redeemed in heaven are male virgins, doubtless a symbol for believers' purity of devotion to Christ. In one of many heavenly promises expressed in the book of Revelation, those who enter heaven will become "a pillar in the temple of my God" (3:12 NIV), a symbolic rather than factual picture.

Later writers also felt free to use symbols to embody qualities of heaven without intending them as literal pictures or analogies. Dante pictured heaven as a gigantic white rose. Milton perpetuated the biblical image of heaven's being foursquare. Bunyan's heaven is bordered by a symbolic river of death, and the joy of entrance into it is symbolized by bells ringing all over the city.

The principle at work here has been stated by C. S. Lewis as a symbolic attempt to express the inexpressible (*Mere Christianity* 106). The passage from Lewis is so full of common sense that it deserves to be quoted:

> All the scriptural imagery (harps, crowns, gold, etc.) is, of course, a merely symbolical attempt to express the inexpressible. Musical instruments are mentioned because for many people (not all) music is the thing known in the present life which most strongly suggests ecstasy and infinity. Crowns are mentioned to suggest the fact that those who are united with God in eternity share His splendour and power and joy. Gold is mentioned to suggest the timelessness of Heaven (gold does not rust) and the preciousness of it. People who take these symbols literally might as well think that when Christ told us to be like doves, he meant that we were to lay eggs.

Postbiblical writers do not picture themselves as adding to our literal information about heaven. They are using symbols and fictions to make the reality come alive to us. Literary people use the phrase "symbolic reality" to name the strategy of using symbols to evoke a reality. There is a sense, then, in which writers can portray heaven in terms of all that the human race most desires and imagines to be best.

DISTANCING

One of the things that writers who have portrayed heaven have done best and most evocatively is to distance heaven from our own experience.

Heaven is literally beyond our known experience. So writers describe it as physically and spiritually remote.

One of their strategies is to build into their stories a sense of increasing expectancy long before we arrive at heaven. Again, C. S. Lewis is particularly good on the subject, this time in a discussion of the gradual approach to Paradise in Milton's *Paradise Lost:* "In this kind of poetry the poet's battles are mainly won in advance. If he can give us the idea of increasing expectancy, the idea of the Paradisal light coming but not yet come, then, when at last he has to make a show of describing . . . , we shall be already conquered" (*A Preface to "Paradise Lost"* 49).

The most frequently used device of distancing in the literature of pilgrimage is to make the reader travel a long distance before arriving at heaven, just as the pilgrim in the story does. Vertical imagery of height and ascent has also been very common. Another technique is to protect heaven from direct approach by barriers of one kind or another. In the medieval poem *Pearl* and in Bunyan's *Pilgrim's Progress,* heaven is separated from mortals by a river. Images of veiling have been prominent. Another common technique is to have characters in the story talk about heaven before the pilgrim (and we) arrive there, in effect giving us an indirect portrayal of it. What all of these techniques have in common is that they distance heaven from direct view and in the process achieve a suggestion of its perfection.

In another variation on the theme, writers assert that heaven is a more advanced or brighter reality of something that we can glimpse on earth, which can give us only a foreshadowing. Dante, for example, pictures heavenly radiance as a river of light in which early glimpses of it "are the shadowy prefaces of the reality," preparing the pilgrim to rise "higher in the divine radiance." At the end of *The Last Battle,* C. S. Lewis portrays earthly life as the cover and title page of a book, and heaven as the chapters ahead. These attempts to distance heaven all suggest its uniqueness while creating a simultaneous anticipation—a longing to arrive there and discover for ourselves the as yet unexplored region which is our heart's desire.

THE IMAGERY OF HEAVEN

Writers who portray heaven gravitate toward predictable types of imagery. I have already noted the prevalence of enameled imagery—

imagery combining brilliance of light and hardness of texture to suggest a world whose glory and permanence transcend our cyclic vegetative world. It is a rare vision of heaven that does not have its quota of gold, jewelry, fiery gems, and a dazzling brightness that goes beyond earthly experience.

Another category of images is conceptual imagery—words that name abstract qualities instead of sensations. The principle involved here is that if heaven transcends the sensory world around us, we should use terminology that rises above the sensory. The medieval mystic St. Dionysius put it succinctly in a comment about the portrayal of God: "Is He not more truly Life and Goodness than air and stone" (*Theologia* 31)? Visions of heaven will almost inevitably have an abundance of words like joy and bliss and peace. Bunyan's Christian is told that in heaven he "will be clothed with glory and majesty."

When writers *do* talk about the objects of heaven, they often use generic imagery—words that name whole categories without giving specific details. The result is to distance heaven from direct view and to achieve some of the same effects as conceptual imagery. In the book of Revelation we read repeatedly about an unspecified "throne," a "tree of life with twelve kinds of fruit," a city with "a great, high wall," and white robes, but in none of these instances are we given a specific picture of the objects. In Bunyan's vision, glorified saints are "put into equipage fit to ride out with the King of glory," but we are given no specific picture of that equipage.

Another tendency among writers is to portray heaven in nonvisual sensory terms, on the logic that sound and smell are less tangible and therefore more appropriate to a heaven that transcends earthly reality. The master image is without doubt musical harmony. Most visions of heaven make it a place of singing and the music of such instruments as harps and trumpets. If we can trust the visions of the authors discussed in this book, heaven will be a musician's paradise.

A final category of imagery is nonempirical images—images that we do not experience on earth. In Milton's heaven, for example, we encounter such nonempirical phenomena as a tree of life, a fount of life, and a river of bliss. Upon entering heaven, Bunyan's pilgrims were "transfigured" and "had raiment put on that shone like gold," obviously different from earthly garments. The angels in Dante's heaven "all had faces of living flames."

THE EFFECTS OF HEAVEN

A final technique by which to portray heaven is to internalize the effects of heaven in either the pilgrim who catches sight of heaven or the actual citizens of heaven. The premise is that heaven is knowable partly by how it satisfies and delights the person or angel who resides there.

The angels in Milton's heaven, for example, "received beatitude [blessedness] past utterance" as they beheld God. As Dante's pilgrim nears the goal of his quest, he tells us that he "ended . . . within myself," speaking of "the sweetness . . . distilled within my heart." When the two Shining Ones initiate Bunyan's Christian into the glories that await him in heaven, they define heaven partly in terms of its effects: "There your eyes shall be delighted with seeing, and your ears with hearing the pleasant voice of the Mighty One." In short, heaven is knowable partly by how it is experienced.

SUMMARY

The techniques by which writers have portrayed heaven should not be dismissed as mere fictions. For the most part, these techniques are used because they portray the actual realities of heaven. Except for obviously symbolic images, our tendency should be to grant literal validity to these techniques.

When Christian physician Richard Eby entered a coma after an accident and experienced a preview of heaven, the experience resembled virtually everything that the poets and visionaries through the centuries had pictured it as being (Eby 197–208). He was overwhelmed with a sense of peace and absence of pain. His body was recognizably his, yet transparent. He was aware of God's presence everywhere. His senses were heightened, the light dazzled him, and a pastoral landscape beyond anything on earth presented itself to his vision.

As the biblical writers themselves show us, literary means are not only the best and truest but often the only means of enabling us to grasp what we may of the kingdom of heaven, the Celestial City, our ultimate home.

WORKS CITED

Calvin, John. *Theological Treatises*. Translated by J. K. S. Reid. Philadelphia: Westminster, 1954.

Dionysius. *The "Theologia" of Saint Dionysius.* Edited by Alan W. Watts. West Park, New York: Holy Cross, 1944.

Eby, Richard E. *Caught Up into Paradise.* Old Tappan, N.J.: Revell, 1978.

Lewis, C. S. *Mere Christianity.* New York: Macmillan, 1943.

———. *A Preface to "Paradise Lost."* New York: Oxford Univ. Press, 1942.

ST. AUGUSTINE'S
CITY OF GOD AND THE
POSTMODERN PILGRIMAGE

BY GENE EDWARD VEITH

S t. Augustine is one of the few theologians claimed by both Catholics and Protestants. Roman Catholics consider him not only a saint, but a "Doctor of the Church" for his foundational work as a Christian theologian and philosopher. But he is also foundational for Protestantism. Luther, an Augustinian monk, used Augustine against medieval scholasticism in teaching that salvation is sheerly through the grace of God. Calvinists insist that their doctrines of election and predestination are not exclusively "Calvinist" but that they are all to be found in Augustine. Evangelicals of all persuasions appreciate him for his "born-again" experience, which he recounts in the *Confessions*, the story of his conversion—his spiritual pilgrimage—that amounts to a profound "personal testimony."

Augustine, who lived from A.D. 354–430, has been called the greatest intellect of the early church. He championed orthodox Christianity against pagan religions and secular philosophers outside the church and, perhaps more importantly, against heretics within the church. He explored spiritual issues with psychological honesty and intellectual rigor, and his insights would influence Christians for centuries to come.

Augustine was an African. He was born in Numidia, educated in Carthage, and after his conversion served as bishop of Hippo, all regions of northern Africa, in present-day Algeria. Augustine apparently sprang from Berber stock, the same nomads that live in northern Africa today. Perhaps Augustine's African identity might win him new attention today among those who decry Eurocentrism and who seek to explore the contributions of non-Europeans to world civilization. But there is another reason Augustine deserves our special attention now in what is being called the postmodern era, our age of moral relativism, cultural determinism, and rejection of every kind of absolute truth. Augustine was writing for an era much like our own, a time of cultural collapse.

In A.D. 410, the city of Rome fell to the barbarians. The city that had gone from a small, creative republic to a world empire was sacked by Alaric and his Goths. Rome, for all of its faults, had brought order, law, and classical civilization throughout the empire. Now the Roman world was falling apart.

Rome had brutally persecuted Christianity until the conversion of Emperor Constantine about a hundred years earlier. Although most of the Roman world remained pagan, Christianity was not only legal, it enjoyed the patronage of the emperors. Many Christians worried that the fall of Rome would mean the fall of Christianity.

Many Christians today are similarly disoriented at our culture's seeming collapse—its rejection of moral truth, its violence and promiscuity, its repudiation of the Christian worldview. Can the church survive, we wonder, in a non-Christian culture?

The pagans of Augustine's time raised another issue: Look what happened when Rome abandoned its ancient gods for this new religion. Later apologists for paganism—such as Sir Edward Gibbon in his Enlightenment-era *Rise and Fall of the Roman Empire*—blamed Christianity for the fall of Rome. A pagan revival, they argued, sponsored by the social and intellectual elite of what remained of the Roman world, began to attack Christianity more aggressively, and the old religions came back in vogue.

In the same way, many people today, disillusioned by the failures of Western civilization, are blaming Christianity for all of its ills. From the West's alleged insensitivity to the environment to the oppressions of "racism, sexism, and homophobia," Christianity is held responsible for the whole range of postmodern evils. Eastern religions, goddess worship, and New Age philosophies are being hailed as liberating alternatives, amounting to a new pagan revival.

In response to the charge that Christianity was to blame for the fall of Rome and in order to deal with the crisis faced by the church with the collapse of Roman civilization, Augustine wrote his greatest theological treatise, *The City of God*. In it, he contrasts the Earthly City—represented supremely by Rome but encompassing all other human cultures—with the Heavenly City, which finds its culmination in heaven but which exists on earth among the church and in the hearts of those who have faith in Christ. The City of God, according to Augustine, corresponds to no earthly institution—not even the visible church, which contains hypocrites and nonbelievers. The City of God is a spiritual community, which must live and work in the Earthly City in a state of pilgrimage.

Augustine's book *The City of God* is itself a pilgrimage, a journey through pagan mythology, Greek philosophy, and Roman culture, moving on through biblical history, from Genesis through Revelation, from the creation of the universe through its redemption in Jesus Christ to the end of time. This spiritual pilgrimage of God's people through a vale of temptation, suffering, and unshakable joy is the subject of *The City of God*. In his most famous book, *The Confessions*, Augustine recounts this pilgrimage in terms of his own life, his personal search for God that made him a part of the Heavenly City. Augustine explores the pilgrimage of both the individual and the church as a whole in a way that is startlingly relevant to the struggles of contemporary Christians.

THE EARTHLY CITY, THEN AND NOW

"For my own part," said C. S. Lewis, "I tend to find the doctrinal books often more helpful in devotion than the theological books. . . . I believe that many who find that 'nothing happens' when they sit down, or kneel down, to a book of devotion, would find that the heart sings unbidden while they are working their way through a tough bit of theology with a pipe in their teeth and a pencil in their hand" ("On the Reading of Old Books"). This is a good description of reading Augustine. *The City of God* is a massive work—the Penguin paperback translation has 1,091 pages—filled with arcane lore from the fifth century, multiple chapters exploring a single verse of Scripture, logical refutations of long-forgotten thinkers, and jaw-dropping spiritual insights. Working your way through Augustine may seem to be a daunting task—I first read *The City of God* as an ambitious Lenten project of mortifying my flesh!—but he can make "the heart sing." Reading *The City of God* seems at first like entering a labyrinth, full of digressions and meandering paths. But like most meandering paths, they go by memorable sites along the way, and they lead to an important destination.

Augustine classifies the citizens of the two cities according to what they love: "We see then that the two cities were created by two kinds of love: the earthly city was created by self-love reaching the point of contempt for God, the Heavenly City by the love of God carried as far as contempt for self" (14.28.593). Augustine is thus interested in both the objective dimension of the two cities and in the subjective dimension—the theological status of the saved as opposed to the lost and to the psychology of both sin and faith.

"The earthly city glories in itself, the Heavenly City glories in the Lord" (14.28.593). The Earthly City is wholly focused on this world, in terms of which its motivations and its values can all be understood. The Heavenly City, on the other hand, though it coexists within the Earthly City, is focused on the transcendent God, who calls out His elect from the sinful world, redeems them in Christ, and sanctifies them with His Holy Spirit. Augustine is not really constructing a theological system; rather, he is creating a structure for discernment, one that allows for both secular analysis and spiritual understanding.

Part of Augustine's task in dealing with the fall of Rome was immediately practical. Many of the issues he deals with were urgent questions raised by a catastrophe that makes our contemporary problems seem trivial. Did the nuns who were raped by the Goths violate their vows of celibacy? (No, he assures them, since there can be no sin without consent of the will.) What about the Christians who were slaughtered by the barbarians in such numbers that their bodies were not given proper burial? (Funerals, he explains, are for the comfort of the living, not a necessity for the dead, whose souls still live and whose bodies will rise again at the Resurrection). Part of his purpose was theoretical, taking on the whole range of classical culture—its history, science, philosophy, and religion—in light of Christian revelation.

To read *The City of God* is to plunge oneself into the ancient world, seeing its accomplishments and its failures, its brutality and its grandeur from the inside. In fact, to read *The City of God* is to acquire a classical education. But in the midst of all of the ancient history, the contemporary reader will experience a shock of recognition.

Consider, for example, the following passage, which demonstrates Augustine's knack for unveiling the psychology of human sinfulness:

> For why is it that you put the blame on this Christian era, when things go wrong? Is it not because you are anxious to enjoy your vices without interference, and to wallow in your corruption, untroubled and unrebuked? For if you are concerned for peace and general prosperity, it is not because you want to make decent use of these blessings, with moderation, with restraint, with self-control, with reverence. No! It is because you seek an infinite variety of pleasure with a crazy extravagance, and your prosperity produces a moral corruption far worse than all the fury of an enemy. (1.30.42)

People who are indignant in the face of hardship because they want to enjoy their vices undisturbed, who are obsessed with prosperity so that nothing can interfere with their mad pursuit of infinite varieties of pleasure—is Augustine describing ancient Romans or contemporary Americans?

Augustine's dissection of the City of Rome is, in fact, an analysis of all sinful human cultures. But because he is focusing on a civilization at its moment of crisis and apparent dissolution, his analysis has a powerful resonance for readers today, when we too—though far less dramatically—are facing a similar cultural meltdown. What is amazing, though, is that Augustine actually anticipates contemporary issues, ideas, and philosophies.

Consider Augustine's description of the two cities in the context of human cultures:

> Although there are many great people throughout the world, living under different customs in religion and morality and distinguished by a complex variety of languages, arms, and dress, it is still true that there have come into being only two main divisions, as we may call them, in human society: and we are justified in following the lead of our Scriptures and calling them two cities. There is, in fact, one city of men who choose to live by the standard of the flesh, another of those who choose to live by the standard of the spirit. (14.1.547)

Augustine seems to be invoking today's language of multiculturalism. Although he recognizes the great diversity of the human race, there are only two categories that really matter: the saved and the lost.

Augustine focuses on the different "standards," the different criteria for determining values, that people use to govern their lives. "Some live by man's standard, others by God's" (14.4.553). The citizen of the Earthly City follows the standard of the flesh, which means "living by the rule of self, that is by the rule of man" (14.3.552). The citizen of the Heavenly City follows the standard of the spirit, which means living "by the standard of his creator, not by his own, carrying out not his own will, but his creator's" (14.4.552).

This sort of talk should sound familiar to a modern reader. We are often told today to live according to our own standards. Existentialist philosophy, values clarification exercises, pop psychology, and television talk shows all encourage us to choose our own moral values, to find out what's right for us, and to live up to the standards we create for ourselves. Augustine acknowledges that this is in fact what we do, but, according to him, "living by our own standards" is the definition of sin and a description of what it means to be lost. Citizens of the Heavenly City, in contrast, do not set their own standards; they accept God's. They do not choose their own values; they follow God's will, not their own. Their principles are based not on the needs of the culture, nor on their own self-interests, nor on their quest for self-fulfillment, but on the revelation of the transcendent God.

Point by point, Augustine anticipates contemporary thought, but then relegates this way of thinking to the sinful condition of the Earthly City. Cynical postmodernists are saying that the real root of culture is power, that all cultural institutions are nothing more than masks that cover up and justify one group's desire to dominate others. Augustine seems to concur when he says that the Earthly City is characterized by "the lust for domination" (14.28.593). Religion, say some social scientists, is primarily a means of social control. Augustine says the same thing about false religions, citing the complicity of human leaders with demons to deceive the people and thus "bring them under control and keep them there" (4.32.176).

According to Augustine, the citizens of the Earthly City may well be very religious. But this religion has a different focus and a different motive from that of the Heavenly City:

> And this is the characteristic of the earthly city—to worship a god or gods so that with their assistance it may reign in the enjoyment of victories and an earthly peace, not with a loving concern for others, but with lust for domination over them. For the good make use of this world to enjoy God, whereas the evil want to make use of God in order to enjoy the world. (15.7.604)

Today's churches that emphasize a gospel of "health and wealth," Augustine would say, belong to the Earthly City. They are trying to use God to enjoy the world. Citizens of the Heavenly City, on the other hand, use the world to enjoy God.

Today's postmodernists are saying that truth is relative, that knowledge is constructed by cultural forces and individual choices and that, therefore, absolute truth is unattainable. The late Roman philosophers were saying much the same thing. "As for that characteristic which Varro produces as the distinctive mark of the New Academy, the view that everything is uncertain," says Augustine, "the City of God roundly condemns such doubt as being madness" (19.18.879).

Unlike the Earthly City, the City of God has a basis for truth. "In matters apprehended by the mind and the reason, it has most certain knowledge," rejoins Augustine. "It also trusts the evidence of the senses in every matter." Above all, the City of God finds truth in the Holy Scriptures (19.18.879). Augustine admits, however, that because of the limits of the human mind, our knowledge is partial, flawed, and incomplete. But even the marvels that we can never understand, with which the world is full, are no evidence that the universe is irrational. "A portent," he points out, "does not occur contrary to nature, but contrary to what is known of nature" (21.8.980). "The almighty does not act irrationally in cases where the feeble human mind cannot give a rational explanation" (21.5.973).

Truth exists, but the problem is that the Earthly City is in rebellion against that truth:

> So when man lives by the standard of truth he lives not by his own standard, but by God's. For it is God who has said, "I am the truth." By contrast, when he lives by his own standard, that is by man's and not by God's standard, then inevitably he lives by the standard of falsehood. (14.4.552)

For all of its sophistication, power, and prosperity, the Earthly City, attempting to live by its own self-created standards, is doomed to futility. Ironically, contemporary thinkers are agreeing with Augustine that culture rests on power, that it asserts its own truths and sets its own standards. What contemporary thinkers do not know, however, is that there is an alternative: The City of God.

THE PILGRIMAGE OF THE CITY OF GOD

The Heavenly City, however, is not a counterculture. "In truth, those two cities are interwoven and intermixed in this era" (1.35.46). A Christian may be a citizen of the Heavenly City, but that city is, literally, in heaven. Those who live on earth are inevitably part of the Earthly City. Those who have their citizenship in heaven must still live in a fallen world, struggling with the evils of society and their own propensity to sin. Augustine explains the relationship between the two cities in terms of a pilgrimage. "The City of God," says Augustine, "is in pilgrimage in this world" (1.35.45).

The City of God includes all of God's elect and is manifested in the church, but the Heavenly City cannot be fully identified with any earthly institution—not even the visible church. "While the City of God is in pilgrimage in this world, she has in her midst some who are united with her in participation in the sacraments, but who will not join with her in the eternal destiny of the saints" (1.35.45). The Heavenly City is the church triumphant, the whole company of the redeemed in heaven, but the visible church on earth includes hypocrites and nominal Christians. The institutional church, as such, is not the City of God.

Conversely, among even the enemies of Christianity are those who will later be converted to faith in Jesus Christ. "The pilgrim City of Christ the King . . . must bear in mind that among these very enemies are hidden her future citizens; and when confronted with them she must not think it a fruitless task to bear with their hostility until she finds them confessing the faith. . . . Some predestined friends, as yet unknown even to themselves, are concealed among our most open enemies" (1.35.45).

The true, invisible church is not some earthly culture; rather, it consists of people from all cultures:

> While this Heavenly city, therefore, is on pilgrimage in this world, she calls out citizens from all nations and so collects a society of aliens, speaking all

36

languages. She takes no account of any difference in customs, laws, and institutions, by which earthly peace is achieved and preserved—not that she annuls or abolishes any of those, rather, she maintains them and follows them (for whatever divergences there are among the diverse nations, those institutions have one single aim—earthly peace). (19.17.878)

The City of God on earth is "a society of aliens," not at home in this world, but participating in it nevertheless. "It is completely irrelevant to the Heavenly City," insists Augustine, "what dress is worn or what manner of life adopted by each person who follows the faith that is the way to God, provided that these do not conflict with the divine instructions" (19.19.879). The Christian church has been called the one truly multicultural institution, consisting of believers from nearly every race, language, and tribe. Augustine would agree and then go further, insisting that while human beings have their cultures, the City of God is not a culture at all, but a transcendent society grounded in the love of God.

"God's City lives in this world's city," explains Augustine, "but it lives there as an alien sojourner" (18.1.761). Although the two cities are spiritually opposed to each other, they coexist side by side. "The two cities, the earthly and the Heavenly, . . . are mingled together from the beginning to the end of their history" (18.54.842).

Citizens of the Heavenly City suffer the same hardships and pursue some of the same goals as their worldly neighbors. "Both cities alike enjoy the good things, or are afflicted with the adversities of this temporal state, but with a different faith, a different expectation, a different love" (18.54.842). Christians are as likely to experience suffering and hardship—or for that matter good fortune—as non-Christians. The difference is the use they make of their sufferings and joys. For the worldly, suffering and joy drive them farther from God. For the spiritual, suffering and joy drive them closer to God.

By the same token, since both Christians and non-Christians have the same physical needs, "both kinds of households alike make use of the things essential for this mortal life, but each has its own very different end in making use of them" (19.17.877). The ultimate goal of both cities is peace—for the Earthly City, the peace of this world, with its personal comfort, prosperity, and security; for the Heavenly City, the peace of eternal life. But the citizens of the Heavenly City have a legitimate interest in earthly peace as well:

The Heavenly City—or rather that part of it which is on pilgrimage in this condition of mortality, and which lives on the basis of faith—must needs make use of this peace also, until this mortal state, for which this kind of peace is essential, passes away. And therefore, it leads what we may call a life of captivity in this earthly city as in a foreign land, although it has already received the promise of redemption, and the gift of the Spirit as a kind of pledge of it; and yet it does not hesitate to obey the laws of the earthly city by which those things which are designed for the support of this mortal life are regulated; and the purpose of this obedience is that, since this mortal condition is shared by both cities, a harmony may be preserved between them in things that are relevant to this condition. (19.17.877)

The Earthly City may be bound by sin; "however, it would be incorrect to say that the goods which this city desires [such as peace, justice, and prosperity] are not goods, since even that city is better, in its own human way, by their possession" (15.4.599).

Citizens of the Heavenly City may thus participate in the life of the Earthly City and may follow its various modes of life, whether a life of leisure, action, or even rule. The difference, again, is in the way they use their secular vocation: in the selfish pursuit of pleasure, honor, and power; or in the spirit of love, justice, and service (19.19.880).

Those whose citizenship is in the City of God do have a foretaste of eternal life even in this world. "They possess the peace of God even now, giving joy amidst wretchedness" (19.7.892). Although they live by God's standards and are sanctified by the Holy Spirit, they still must struggle with temptation and sin. Since they are not saved by their works but by the grace of God through Jesus Christ, their righteousness, "though genuine," consists not in "the perfection of virtues" but in the forgiveness of sins (19.27.892).

Augustine manages to be both practical and otherworldly. He is realistic about both the evils of this world and the necessity to work in its terms. He is idealistic in his conviction that ultimate reality is to be found not in the transience of this life but in the transcendent, eternal realm of the spirit. At the same time, his idealism also extends to this world, in which God's providence governs every detail of human history. According to Augustine, Christians can neither avoid the world nor conquer it; they must engage the world, while being aware that the world will pass away. This is what it means to be in a state of pilgrimage. "Scripture tells us that

Cain [the type of the ungodly] founded a city," observes Augustine, "whereas Abel, as a pilgrim, did not found one. For the City of the saints is up above, although it produces citizens here below, and in their persons the City is on pilgrimage until the time of its kingdom comes" (15.1.596).

AUGUSTINE'S PILGRIMAGE

In his *Confessions*, Augustine describes his own pilgrimage from the Earthly City to the Heavenly City, from sin and unbelief to faith in Christ and the love of God. This first autobiography in world literature is in the form of a long prayer to God, to whom the whole work is addressed. It is thus, quite literally, Augustine's "confession," his laying out his life and his sin before God, who grants him forgiveness.

The opening of the *Confessions* sums up every pilgrimage: "Thou madest us for Thyself, and our heart is restless, until it repose in Thee" (1.3). Both the Earthly City and the Heavenly City seek peace; the difference is where they look to find it. Throughout the *Confessions*, Augustine describes himself looking to the world for what he can truly find only in God. Every moment of ordinary life becomes a trial in his pilgrimage.

As he tells about his education and his career, the ideas that he was flirting with and the sins that were entangling him, we see a portrait of the citizen of the Earthly City. His standards were his own. At the same time, he experienced the contradictions and the futility of trying to find peace apart from God. "I loathed exceedingly to live and feared to die," he said in words that anticipate today's angst-ridden secularists (4.60). Augustine's particular problem was with sexual sins. Carthage—in another parallel to our time—was notorious for its sexual promiscuity. Augustine took up with a mistress, had an illegitimate son, and gave free rein to his sexual desires.

As a result of his mother's prayers, his meeting the great Christian teacher St. Ambrose, the conversion of a friend, and other influences, Augustine began to see the truth of Christianity. In the ultimate example, however, of a perverse and earthly will, Augustine resisted giving in to what he knew to be true because he did not want to give up his sexual vices. He prayed, "Give me chastity and continency, only not yet." He was afraid "lest Thou shouldest hear me soon, and soon cure me of the disease of concupiscence, which I wished to have satisfied, rather than extinguished" (8.158).

One day he was in a garden. He heard a child in a neighboring house chanting, for some reason, "Take up and read; take up and read." Picking up a Bible, he opened it at random and read: "Let us walk honestly, as in the day; not in rioting and drunkenness, not in chambering and wantonness, not in strife and envying: But put ye on the Lord Jesus Christ, and make not provision for the flesh, to fulfill the lusts thereof" (Romans 13:13–14 KJV). "Instantly at the end of this sentence," recalls Augustine, "by a light as it were of serenity infused into my heart, all the darkness of doubt vanished away" (8.167).

This encounter with God's Word made him a Christian. He was baptized, as was his fifteen-year-old illegitimate son. In Book 9 of the *Confessions*, Augustine describes both his baptism and the death of his mother, Monica. His father had been a pagan, but his mother was a devout Christian. Throughout his life, she desperately prayed for her son. Shortly before she died, her prayers were answered. In fact, she saw her husband become a Christian on his deathbed. In Book 9, the mood of joy at Augustine's coming to faith is tempered somewhat by his grief at the death of his mother, whom he honors with a moving, emotional tribute to her love and to her faith.

The autobiography pretty much ceases after this point, the four remaining books consisting of extraordinary meditations on time and the creation. Augustine was thirty-three when he became a Christian, and he would live for forty-three more years. But his pilgrimage to the Heavenly City was, in a sense, complete, though he had longer to sojourn in this world.

THE CITY OF HEAVEN

Augustine writes about his pilgrimage as a search for God, but toward the end of the *Confessions* he realizes that God has actually been searching for him: He prays to Jesus Christ, "through Whom Thou soughtest us, not seeking Thee, but soughtest us, that we might seek Thee" (11.245). The pilgrimage of human beings from earth to heaven is made possible only by Christ's pilgrimage from heaven to earth. Similarly, toward the end of *The City of God*, Augustine describes the Heavenly City not as a distant goal to strive for but as the finished gift of God. Augustine comments on Revelation 21:2, "Then I saw the great City, the new Jerusalem, coming down out of heaven":

This City has been coming down from heaven since its beginning, from the time when its citizens began to increase in number as they have continued to increase throughout the period of this present age, by the grace of God which comes from above by means of the "washing of rebirth" in the Holy Spirit sent down from heaven. (20.17.928)

The initiative is always God's, and salvation is always by God's grace.

One of the hallmarks of salvation is freedom. This theologian who doubted whether human beings in bondage to sin can be thought to have free will believes that heaven will be a place of perfect freedom. "The will will be the freer in that it is freed from a delight in sin," he writes. "In the Heavenly City then, there will be freedom of will. It will be one and the same freedom in all, and indivisible in the separate individuals. It will be freed from all evil and filled with all good, enjoying unfailingly the delight of eternal joys" (22.30.1089). The beatitude of heaven will not be simply an individual experience, but one involving others. Heaven is described by the Bible and by Augustine as a city, and, as he reminds us, "the life of a city is inevitably a social life" (19.17.879).

THE GOAL OF THE PILGRIMAGE

The highest joy of heaven will be to experience God Himself, for whom our restless hearts have yearned all of our lives: "He will be the goal of all our longings; and we shall see him for ever; we shall love him without satiety; we shall praise him without wearying. This will be the duty, the delight, the activity of all, shared by all who share the life of eternity" (22.30.1088). "There we shall be still and see; we shall see and we shall love; we shall love and we shall praise. Behold what will be, in the end, without end! For what is our end but to reach that kingdom which has no end?" (22.30.1091).

With these words, *The City of God* concludes, having reached the goal of its pilgrimage. Augustine finished the work, which took him thirteen years to write, in A.D. 426. Soon after, the Vandals—one of the barbarian tribes that trashed the civilization of Rome—moved into northern Africa. They besieged Hippo, the city in which Augustine was a bishop. Augustine lay dying as the Vandals were outside the gates. Eleven months after his death in A.D. 430, the Vandals destroyed the city. But they could not destroy the City of God.

WORKS CITED

St. Augustine. *The City of God.* Translated by Henry Bettenson. New York: Penguin, 1972.

St. Augustine. *The Confessions of Saint Augustine.* Translated by Edward B. Pusey. New York: Modern Library, 1949.

FURTHER READING

What Augustine said of the Roman academician Varro could be said of Augustine himself: He was "a man who read so much that we marvel that he had any time for writing; who wrote so much that we find it hard to believe that anyone could have read it all" (*The City of God* 6.2.230). His works take up the first eight volumes of the mammoth edition of *The Nicene and Post-Nicene Fathers of the Christian Church*, and they have inspired hundreds of commentators and scholarly studies. Here are some starting points for further reading, focusing on *The City of God*, the *Confessions*, and introductions to his thought.

Works by St. Augustine
Basic Writings of Saint Augustine. 2 vols. Edited by Whitney J. Oates. Grand Rapids: Baker, 1993.
The City of God. Translated by Henry Bettenson. New York: Penguin, 1972.
The City of God. Translated by Marcus Dods. New York: Modern Library, 1950.
The Confessions of Saint Augustine. Translated by Edward B. Pusey. New York: Modern Library, 1949.
Confessions of St. Augustine. Edited by Hal Helms. Modern English Version. Springfield, Mo.: Paraclete, 1986.
The Essential Augustine. Edited by Vernon J. Bourke. New York: New American Library, 1964.
The Nicene and Post-Nicene Fathers of the Christian Church. Edited by Philip Schaff. First Series. Grand Rapids: Eerdmans, 1974. Vols. 1–8.

Works About St. Augustine
Battenhouse, Roy Wesley, ed. *A Companion to the Study of St. Augustine.* Grand Rapids: Baker, 1979.

Bourke, Vernon. *Wisdom from St. Augustine.* Houston, Tex.: Center for Thomistic Studies, 1984.

Brown, Peter. *Augustine of Hippo: A Biography.* Berkeley: Univ. of California Press, 1967.

Guitton, Jean. *The Modernity of Saint Augustine.* Translated by A. V. Littledale. Baltimore: Helicon, 1959.

Markus, R. A. *Saeculum: History and Society in the Theology of St. Augustine.* Cambridge: Cambridge Univ. Press, 1988.

Marshall, Michael. *The Restless Heart: The Life and Influence of St. Augustine.* Grand Rapids: Eerdmans, 1987.

McMahon, Robert. *Augustine's Prayerful Ascent: An Essay on the Literary Form of the "Confessions."* Athens, Ga.: Univ. of Georgia Press, 1989.

Neuhaus, Richard John, ed. *Augustine Today.* Grand Rapids: Eerdmans, 1993.

THREE

DANTE'S VISION OF HEAVEN

BY BARBARA REYNOLDS

Some people believe that Dante had an actual vision of God.[1] It is thought that this occurred in 1300, the year of the Papal Jubilee, when, at the age of thirty-five, he visited Rome. In accordance with this belief, Dante's allegorical poem, *The Divine Comedy*, was the result of his mystical experience and represents in narrative form the steps by which such a vision might be recaptured and understood.

Whether this is true or not, Dante's picture of heaven is presented as the final stage of a threefold journey. *Inferno, Purgatory,* and *Paradise* are three places or states of the soul and mind through which the narrator and, with him, the reader gradually progress. It is an intellectual as well as a spiritual journey, from the surrender of sin to an eager anticipation of heaven. The process can be described as the gradual shedding of error. With the opening of the mind comes the opening of the heart. With enlightenment comes amazement. Doubt, bewilderment, and despair give way to certainty, clarity, and joy. The deeper the horror at the revelation of evil, the more radiant the recognition of divine goodness. This is the staggering paradox of Dante's concept of heaven and a continuing challenge to the reader.

FREEDOM OF THE WILL

Underpinning the structure of the whole poem is the freedom of the will. This, one of the work's most powerful affirmations, is stressed again and again. Dante knew about the influence of heredity and environment, though he did not speak of them in modern terms; he recognized them as part of destiny but insisted that the individual will is free. Damnation is the soul's persistent refusal to acknowledge sin and to seek the forgiveness of God: this is the story of *Inferno*. Repentance and readiness to make reparation, leading to the renewal of the right relationship with God: that is the story of *Purgatory*. Freedom to choose between these two is the glory of the human condition.

Yet, despite all that he sees and learns on the first two stages of his pilgrimage, Dante (as he presents himself in the narrative) is still not prepared for what he finds in heaven. The whole of the third stage is a further shedding of error, a willingness to relinquish misconceptions which remain and to replace them by the truth. Dante has still much to learn, and he delights in doing so. This delight, which he shares with the reader, is the pulsation and momentum of the poem.

Dante's guide through hell had been Virgil, the poet-sage of ancient Rome, who came near to apprehending Christ, yet could not reach so far.[2] In *Purgatory*, Virgil often finds himself at a loss and other mentors are at hand to enlighten Dante on predestination, free will, and salvation by Christ. Through *Paradise*, his guide is Beatrice. She is the Florentine girl he knew and loved in his youth, who had seemed to him then to embody all perfection; but here, beyond yet somehow not apart from her personal self, she is also the truth which Dante seeks. Continually he asks her for explanation, reassurance, and guidance. Continually he receives illumination until, "like a star in Heaven, the truth is seen." *Paradise* is an unending question-and-answer dialogue, reinforced by an unfolding series of visions, until the final vision, in which, in a dazzling moment of illumination, the final question is answered and understood: what is God's relation to the universe and humanity's relation to God? Yet not even the powers of Beatrice suffice for this peak revelation. She is replaced at this point by St. Bernard of Clairvaux, the mystic contemplative who in his first life (that is, life on earth) had a vision of God. He prays that Dante too, still in the first life, may behold God. The prayer is granted, and there the story of the journey ends.

THE GRACE OF GOD IN DANTE'S VISION

By his own free will, Dante chooses to liberate his mind from error and to open his soul to the truth, but he takes no credit to himself for this. Again and again he makes plain that he is the recipient of divine grace. In the famous opening of *Inferno*, he describes himself as lost in a dark wood. By heavenly grace, Virgil is sent to help him—Virgil, by whose pagan wisdom he can still be reached. Defeated by an awareness of his own error and by a sense of his helplessness in the power of evil, Dante is near despair. What escape is there? None, says Virgil, except to come face-to-face with the reality of sin and, having recognized it, to reject it.

As a young poet, Dante Alighieri of Florence had glimpsed the possibility of joy. A follower of the school of courtly love, he believed in the revelation of perfection in beauty, and his early poems to Beatrice and other women are an expression of this idealism. In his own life he fell short of perfection, and he later felt remorse for this. He experienced combat in battle, political intrigue, civil war, and, in 1302, exile from home, family, and possessions. Thereafter he lived on the charity of patrons, a political refugee, looking on at the disintegration of civic decency and freedom, not only in Florence but in other Italian cities. He had hopes for the restoration of order and authority, but they were disappointed. He had no difficulty in recognizing evil. His picture of hell is based on experience. The astonishing thing is that he also envisaged heaven.

DANTE'S CAPACITY FOR JOY

Chesterton wisely concludes that "praise should be the permanent pulsation of the soul" (orthodoxy). Despite disillusionment and the tragedy of his own life, Dante the mature man never lost his youthful capacity for joy. As the poet of *Paradise*, he exploits to the full his powers to communicate it, demonstrating his wonderment at all he sees and hears. His journey through heaven, based on pre-Copernican understanding of the universe, takes the form of an ascent through the heavenly spheres, which carry in their circling round the earth the seven planets (as then identified) and the "fixed" stars.

47

He enters first the Heaven of the Moon, and there experiences his earliest revelation of the nature of celestial joy. The soul of Piccarda Donati, chosen to represent those whose constancy to vows had been imperfect, sets Dante's bewilderment to rest: are such souls content to be, as it appears to him, less near to God than others? Piccarda's famous reply (Canto 3, lines 64–87), that what God wills is also the will of the souls and that His will is their peace, prepares his mind for what he learns in the Heaven of Mercury (Canto 6) from the soul of the Emperor Justinian, that, however hard it is for us to interpret the lessons of history, God's will and divine justice are one and the same; and for what he later learns in the Heaven of Jupiter (Cantos 18–20) concerning God's plan for us of justice and of peace.

In the Heaven of the Sun (Cantos 10–14), Dante comes into the presence of twenty-four great minds, manifested to him in a double circle of lights and representing the various aspects of God's truth: theologians, philosophers, historians, all those by whom our understanding of the Word has been expounded: St. Thomas Aquinas, Albertus Magnus, Orosius, St. Bonaventure, Bede, St. Anselm, Boethius, Sigier of Brabant . . . and on and on—even the soul of Solomon is present—until their two circles are ringed by yet a third. On earth, often at odds and in conflict with one another, here they symbolize the indivisible truth of God.

Moving in perfect accord, they celebrate as in a joyful festival of dance and song their union of learning and love, of seraphic ardor and cherubic insight. The spheres of heaven whirl, dizzy with delight; the angels and the rejoicing souls weave their fantastic dance; there is laughter, inebriation, a riot of charity.[3] Such is the plenitude of Dante's participation—he hears St. Bonaventure extol St. Francis, and St. Thomas Aquinas praise the feats of St. Dominic—that it is difficult to single out one moment for special comment. Perhaps the most sublime is the response of Solomon to Beatrice's request for Dante's sake for words of enlightenment concerning the resurrection of the body:

> "Long as shall last the feast of Paradise,
> Even so long," it said, "our love shall lace
> This radiance round us for our festal guise.

> Its brightness with our fervour shall keep pace,
> Fervour with sight, sight so enlarge the mesh
> Of its own worth as it hath more of grace;
>
> And when we put completeness on afresh,
> All the more gracious shall our person be,
> Reclothèd in the holy and glorious flesh;
>
> Whereby shall grow the unearned gift and free
> The Highest Good bestows—that gift of light
> By which we are enabled Him to see;
>
> Hence must we ever win to more of sight,
> And by more sight more fervour still acquire,
> And by more fervour radiance still more bright.
>
> (14.37–51)

As Dante, in the body (yet a further source of wonderment, to himself as to us) mounts up through the heavenly spheres, the loveliness of Beatrice increases and his ability to look on her strengthens. In the Heaven of Mars (Cantos 15–17), he experiences a supreme moment of amazement and joy when he comes into the presence of his ancestor, the Crusader Cacciaguida, who foretells his future and fortifies him in his resolution to speak the truth freely. In the Heaven of the Fixed Stars, after a vision of the church triumphant, of the Virgin Mary, and of Christ Himself, Beatrice calls on the souls remaining to admit Dante to their joy:

> "O fellowship of the elect who sup
> With Christ the Lamb, Who doth so nourish you
> That full to overflowing is your cup,
>
> If God by grace admits this man unto
> The broken meats that from your table fall,
> Before the hour prescribed by death is due,
>
> The boundless measure of his love recall.
> Bedew him with some drops! *your* fountainhead,
> Whence comes what *he* thinks, is perpetual."
>
> (24.1–9)

In response, the souls, "each brightly blazing like a comet's head," whirl in a circle, from which one then detaches itself. This is the soul of St. Peter (no less!), the first of three (the others are St. James and St. John) who will examine Dante in the three theological virtues: faith, hope, and love. So well does he acquit himself that, when the interrogations are ended, heaven bursts into a hymn of praise. This is one of the climaxes in the mounting joy of the poem:

> "To Father and to Son and Holy Ghost,"
> All Heaven broke forth, "Be glory!"—such sweet din,
> My sense was drunken to the uttermost;
>
> And all I saw, I thought to see therein
> A smile of all creation; thus through eye
> And ear I drew the inebriate rapture in.
>
> O joy no tongue can tell! O ecstasy!
> O perfect life fulfilled of love and peace!
> O wealth past want, that ne'er shall fade nor fly!"
>
> (27.1–9)

TIME AND ETERNITY

The story of Dante's journey is set in time—very precise time. It begins on Good Friday and ends on the following Wednesday of the year 1300. Above and beyond this temporal framework is a mode of being which words—not even Dante's words—cannot convey but only negatively suggest: "Beyond the measurement of night and day, / beyond all boundary," Dante says, God created the universe and, with it, time (29.16–17). The triune Godhead exists beyond space and time: the concepts "where" and "when" do not apply. Only the blessed share this timelessness. "Eternity," said Boethius, "is the perfect and simultaneous possession of unending life"—unending, not in the meaning of endless prolonging, but in a sense that has no relation to time. The entering into this timelessness is beatitude. This is what happens to Dante during the vision in the last canto of *Paradise*, and perhaps happened to him in his actual life, for it is a revelation which mystics are said to experience.

The same is true of spacelessness, the absence of all notion of "where." Within the story of *Paradise*, the souls appear to Dante in the spheres through which he ascends, but in the timelessness of their beatitude, they do not leave the Empyrean—the "wherelessness" of the Abode of God. Because Dante (and the reader) is in the first life, things are shown to him not in their essence, which is how the blessed see them, but in sequence, that is to say, in time.

Beatrice makes this plain to Dante (and thereby to the reader) in the fourth canto. All the souls, she explains, dwell with God, though they appear to him in different spheres. How else could he apprehend them? He has his mortal limitations. In the same way, she adds, the Bible speaks in picture language about God's "hands" and "feet" and describes archangels as having "faces": none of this is to be taken literally, she comments, but "intending / That you should draw a different inference" (4.37–45). How, then, are we to understand the state of being in heaven, and how does Dante convey it?

THE POWER OF DANTE'S POETRY

"It is a marvel," wrote Dorothy L. Sayers in her first publication on Dante, "to watch mere poetry, mere words, thus go up and up, and to feel such inner certainty that we can trust the poet to take them all the way" ("And Telling You a Story" 35). How does he do it? This is a question which we can scarcely hope to answer, for it is a matter of supreme poetic achievement. But we can identify a number of factors. First, there is the relief to the imagination of being released from the torments of hell and the rigors of purgatory. Second, there is the sensation of ascending, or as Sayers describes it, "the ecstatic flight from circle to circle of the mystic dance which is the joy and freedom of the spirit in the willed surrender of its own self-will" (unpublished letter to Charles Williams). We can also discern rhetorical devices: the professions of inability to express all he saw, the silences, the omissions, as when he sees Beatrice transfigured:

> Were everything I've ever said of her
> Rolled up into a single jubilee,
> Too slight a hymn for this new task were there.
>
> Beauty past knowledge was displayed to me—
> Not only ours: the joy of it complete
> Her Maker knows, I think, and only He.

From this point on I must admit defeat
Sounder than poet wrestling with his theme,
Comic or tragic, e'er was doomed to meet;

For her sweet smile remembered, as the beam
Of sunlight blinds the weakest eyes that gaze,
Bewilders all my wits and scatters them.

(30.16–27)

One of his most daunting tasks was to describe the Empyrean.[4] Before he does so, he prepares the reader by representing himself as blinded by light and then regaining his sight, which is now so strengthened that nothing more can dazzle it. First, he sees a river of light, bordered with flowers. From the stream arise living sparks like rubies set in gold, flying among the blooms. These are but an image of what he is about to see. Beatrice bids him bathe his eyes in the stream. When he has done so, he beholds both courts of heaven, of angels and of human souls:

So, as I looked, to greater joyances
The gems and flowers were changed, and I beheld
Both courts of Heaven in true appearances.

Splendour of God, whereby these eyes beheld
Thy true realm's triumph, grant me power to say
How that exalted triumph I beheld.

(30.94–99)[5]

And there follows the vision of the Celestial Rose (30.100–148). Its size is beyond dimension, and yet, Dante's perception of it is complete. On its petals are seated the souls of the departed, seen now, no longer as lights, as during Dante's ascent through the spheres, but in human semblance. Beatrice exclaims: "Behold how great the white-robed company! / Look on our city, see its gyres full-spread!" (30.129–30). Dante contemplates it, and as he watches, the angels, like a swarm of bees, minister peace and love to the souls of the redeemed:

So now, displayed before me as a rose
Of snow-white purity, the sacred might
I saw, whom with His blood Christ made His spouse.

But the other, winging ever in His sight,
Chants praises to the glory it adores,
Its Maker's good extolling in delight.

As bees ply back and forth, now in the flowers
Busying themselves, and now intent to wend
Where all their toil is turned to sweetest stores,

So did the host of Angels now descend
Amid the Flower of the countless leaves,
Now rise to where their love dwells without end.
(31.1–12)

This is yet another of Dante's methods of describing the unimaginable: he compares it with something familiar. And yet, it is so far from the everyday that he falls into a stupor of amazement and silence. Thus it comes about that he misses the departure of Beatrice (as he missed the departure of Virgil at the top of the mountain of purgatory). When he next turns to her for guidance, she is gone. In her place stands St. Bernard. She has returned to her place in heaven—so far removed, so "whereless," and yet

By no material means made visible
Distinct her image came to me below.
(31.77–78)

And he utters his final words to her:

"O thou in whom my hopes securely dwell,
And who, to bring my soul to Paradise,
Didst leave the imprint of thy steps in Hell,

Of all that I have looked on with these eyes
Thy goodness and thy power have fitted me
Thy holiness and grace to recognize.

Thou has led me, a slave to liberty,
By every path, and using every means
Which to fulfill this task were granted thee.

Keep turned towards me thy munificence
So that my soul which thou hast remedied
May please thee when it quits the bonds of sense."
(31.79–90)

THIS WORLD AND THE NEXT

Our world is never far from the thoughts of the blessed. Untroubled
in their mode of being in eternity, they are nevertheless concerned, within
the mode of time, with life as lived on earth. Since our will is free, it follows that the choice of good is an occasion of rejoicing in heaven and the
choice of evil an occasion of wrath. St. Peter bursts forth into startling
denunciation of Pope Boniface, Beatrice pours scorn on trivial-minded
preachers who substitute their own petty words for those of the Gospel,
and Peter Damian rails against degenerate priests, and his words are greet-
ed by so loud a cry from the souls in the Heaven of Saturn that Dante
falls into a swoon of terror. The tenderness with which Beatrice reassures
him is matched by the deadliness of her prophecy of the punishment that
is destined to fall upon wrongdoers.

Dante had yet to return to earth and live out the rest of his life there.
As it happened, that was not to be for long. Soon after describing his final
vision of God and his sudden understanding of how our human nature is
united by the Incarnation with the Godhead, soon after, that is, he had
written the last words of *Paradise:*

High phantasy lost power and here broke off;
Yet, as a wheel moves smoothly, free from jars,
My will and my desire were turned by love,

The love that moves the sun and the other stars

he set aside pen and paper and hastened to do the bidding of his patron,
Guido the Younger of Ravenna, and went on an embassy to Venice.
Returning, he caught malaria and died before ever writing another word,
or even before he had finally assembled and put in order all the pages of
Paradise.

It is perhaps to be regretted that readers do not begin acquaintance
with Dante by reading *Paradise* first. He is almost always spoken of as the
poet of *Inferno* and only a minority of his readers venture further. Yet *Par-*

adise is his greatest achievement, perhaps one of the greatest achievements in all poetry. The fact that a human mind could imagine heaven as he did and so convey it is itself an indication that it must exist. As Dante himself said, "I know that I beheld it, for as I recall it I rejoice."

In the New Testament, joy marks the life of the early church and accompanies the gift of the Holy Spirit to the disciples. We are commanded to rejoice, to respond actively to what is good. We speak of "a leap of faith." We might also speak of "a leap of love," which makes possible the act of rejoicing. St. Thomas Aquinas said: "Joy is not a virtue but an act of love." He also defined beatitude as experiencing the joy of truth—and this could stand very well also as a definition of Dante's vision of heaven.

NOTES

1. For example, William Anderson, author of *Dante the Maker* (London: Routledge & Kegan Paul, 1980).

2. It was believed that in his 4th Eclogue Virgil had unknowingly foretold the birth of Christ.

3. C. S. Lewis, who knew Dante's poem well, has used the concept of the Great Dance of the universe in the last chapter of *Perelandra*, which is in fact a descant upon *Paradise*.

4. The highest heaven, the Abode of God (though "abode," signifying "place," is an inadequate concept for what is spaceless).

5. Dante uses the word *vidi* ("I beheld") three times in the rhyme position, as though to emphasize that he indeed saw what he describes.

WORKS CITED

Dante Alighieri. *The Divine Comedy*. Translated by Dorothy L. Sayers. 3 vols. New York: Penguin, 1962. Parenthetical references are to canto and line numbers.

Dorothy L. Sayers. "And Telling You a Story." In *Further Papers on Dante*. London: Methuen, 1957.

FURTHER READING

The introduction and notes to Dorothy L. Sayers's translation of Dante's *Divine Comedy* (see above) are the best available for readers who have not yet made the acquaintance of Dante.

John R. Richardson's *An Interview with Dante Alighieri* is an excellent introduction to the relevance of Dante's poem to modern readers. This brief work was printed privately and is available from Professor Julius Scott, Jr., c/o Wheaton College, Wheaton, Illinois, 60187.

Luke, Helen M. *Dark Wood to White Rose.* Pecos, N.M.: Dove, 1975.

Ferguson, Francis. *Dante.* London: Weidenfeld & Nicolson, 1966.

Brandeis, Irma. *The Ladder of Vision: A Study of Dante's "Comedy."* London: Chatto & Windus, 1960.

Ralphs, Sheila. *Etterno Spiro: A Study in the Nature of Dante's Paradise.* Manchester, England: Manchester Univ. Press, 1959.

Nuttall, Geoffrey. *The Faith of Dante Alighieri.* London: S.P.C.K., 1969.

Sayers, Dorothy L. "The Meaning of Heaven and Hell." In *Introductory Papers on Dante.* London: Methuen, 1954.

FOUR

FINDING HEAVEN IN
MILTON'S *PARADISE LOST*

BY LELAND RYKEN

. . . .

John Milton (1608–74), the second greatest English writer (behind Shakespeare), is known as both a poet and a writer of polemical prose. Milton was born into a Puritan home (in fact, Milton's father had been permanently put out of his parental home when his Catholic father found him reading an English Bible in his room). This Puritan family valued education and the arts, and Milton is the most learnéd of English writers. Yet his poetic portrayal of heaven is accessible to anyone who is willing to give it his or her best effort.

THE PURITAN CONTEXT OF
MILTON'S POETRY

The doctrinal context within which to understand Milton is the Puritan movement that tried during the first half of the seventeenth century to purify the Anglican church in England of its remaining vestiges of Roman Catholicism. The cornerstone of Puritan belief in all matters, including the conception of heaven, was that the Bible is the only reliable authority for belief and practice. Another basic assumption of the Puritans was the primacy of the spiritual over the earthly and physical.

Within such a framework, it was only natural that the Puritans wrote and thought much of heaven. They had the Bible to assure them that heaven was important to the Christian faith. A firm belief in heaven, moreover, is the most immediate consequence of believing in the primacy of the spiritual. To this we can add that the Puritans were an often persecuted minority within their own society, and the hope of heaven often shines brightest when earthly prospects are dimmest. It is small wonder that (in the words of one authority on Puritan meditation) "the Puritan literature on heaven is enormous" (Kaufmann 134).

For the Puritans, heaven remained the goal that gave direction to their very active life in this world. Puritan theologian William Perkins believed that "our life on earth is but a pilgrimage, and . . . our desire must be to attain a better country, namely, heaven itself," and "in a word, to make an end of the preface" (1: 333). (The latter metaphor might well remind Narnia lovers of the similar image that C. S. Lewis uses on the last page of *The Last Battle*, with its picture of earthly life as only "the cover and title page," and entry into heaven as "beginning Chapter One of the Great Story, which no one on earth has read: which goes on for ever: in which every chapter is better than the one before.")

The gate that opens the reality of heaven to Christians, the Puritans agreed, is faith. After all, "faith is the substance of things hoped for, the evidence of things not seen" (Hebrews 11:1 KJV). An expected part of the Christian life was thus "to foresee by faith the glory of heaven" (Baxter 130–31). "Heavenly meditation" became a standard Puritan practice, with a view toward the Christian's being raised to heaven "in our affections [emotions] before we be there in our bodies" (Richard Sibbes, quoted in Kaufman 134). Richard Baxter wrote a whole book on cultivating the habit of heavenlymindedness, entitled *The Saints' Everlasting Rest*, a devotional classic to this day.

If the goal of life is to attain heaven, at least two important directives follow for conducting life in this world. One is to keep the goal in constant awareness, viewing earthly life as a preparation. Richard Baxter advised his readers, "Always remember whither you are going; that you are preparing for everlasting rest and joy" (77). Richard Sibbes wrote, "The life of a Christian is wondrously ruled in this world, by the consideration

. . . of the life of another world" (quoted in Kaufmann 134).

The other directive that the Puritans drew from a belief that heaven was the believer's eventual home was to keep earthly endeavors subordinate to the great endeavor. John Preston wrote that "what business so ever we have in the world, . . . our main business is in heaven" (269). Baxter's advice was to "let your life on earth be a conversation in heaven" (153). The Puritans' favorite metaphor to express this view of life was that of the pilgrimage: "When God hath assured to a Christian spirit the inheritance of heaven, he joyfully pilgrims it through this world" (Thomas Adams 1:154).

John Milton absorbed this outlook on life from his Puritan upbringing. In a college oration, Milton wrote:

> This I consider, my hearers, as known and received by all, that the greater Maker of the universe, when he had framed all else fleeting and subject to decay, did mingle with man, in addition to that of him which is mortal, a certain divine breath, immortal, indestructible, free from death and all hurt. . . . ; and I consider, accordingly, that nothing can deservedly be taken into account among the causes of our happiness, unless it somehow or other regards not only this worldly life, but also that life everlasting.

What is important here is the orientation heavenward—an orientation that the modern spirit makes it difficult to attain.

Milton went on to make this orientation the basis of his "poetic"—his philosophy of writing—as articulated most explicitly in a poem entitled "At a Solemn Music." In brief, that philosophy is this: the poet is a seer or prophet who glimpses the harmonious vision of perfection that existed before the Fall and that exists always in heaven. The poet-prophet, equipped and inspired by God, can create a heavenly vision of perfection for readers to share and profit from.

GLIMPSES OF HEAVEN IN MILTON'S EARLY POETRY

An admirer of Milton's poetry began an essay with the comment, "It is as if he were always thinking of Heaven; this is his true subject" (Arthos 90). We can catch glimpses of this already in some of Milton's early poems, which provide a more accessible entrée into Milton's heavenly vision than the big one, *Paradise Lost*.

Consider, for example, a poem written on the occasion of the death of a friend of Milton and entitled "On the Religious Memory of Mrs. Catharine Thomason, My Christian Friend":

> When Faith and Love which parted from thee never,
>> Had ripened thy just soul to dwell with God,
>> Meekly thou didst resign this earthly load
> Of Death, called Life, which us from life doth sever.
>> Thy works and alms and all thy good endeavour
>> Stayed not behind, nor in the grave were trod;
>> But as faith pointed with her golden rod,
>> Followed thee up to joy and bliss forever.
> Love led them on, and faith who knew them best
>> Thy handmaids, clad them o're with purple beams
>> And azure wings, that up they flew so dressed,
> And spoke the truth of thee in glorious themes
>> Before the Judge, who thenceforth bid thee rest
>> And drink thy fill of pure immortal streams.

Behind the poem stand some famous verses from the book of Revelation (especially 14:13, with its assurance regarding those who "rest from their labor" that "their deeds follow them" [NIV]). The movement within the poem is a paradigm of the Christian's life—from the life of faith on earth to everlasting reward in heaven.

For a vision of a saint's life in heaven, we can turn to Milton's dream-vision of his deceased wife, who had died a couple of months after childbirth. Milton begins by comparing his wife's return to him in a vision to the story from classical mythology of a wife who returned to her husband through the efforts of Hercules, and then he paints a picture of his wife as a redeemed saint in heaven:

> Methought I saw my late espoused saint,
>> Brought to me like Alcestis from the grave,
>> Whom Jove's great Son to her glad husband gave,
>> Rescued from death by force, though pale and faint.
> Mine as whom washed from spot of child-bed taint,
>> Purification in the old law did save,
>> And such as yet one more I trust to have
>> Full sight of her in heaven without restraint,

Came vested all in white, pure as her mind;
　　Her face was veiled, yet to my fancied sight,
　　Love, sweetness, goodness, in her person shined
So clear, as in no face with more delight.
　　But O, as to embrace me she inclined,
　　I waked, she fled, and day brought back my night.

In this dream portrait of Milton's wife in heaven we find the embodiment of such Christian realities as redemption, glorification, eternal life, and the numinous or holy. We also experience the sense of separation and longing that separates loved ones on earth from those in heaven, as expressed in the image of the veiled figure.

When Milton became totally blind at the age of forty-three or forty-four, he wrote the following sonnet expressing his anguish over his fear that he would not stand approved in the sight of a God who expected service from His creatures:

When I consider how my light is spent,
　　Ere half my days in this dark world and wide,
　　And that one talent which is death to hide,
　　Lodged with me useless, though my soul more bent
To serve therewith my Maker, and present
　　My true account, lest he returning chide;
　　"Doth God exact day-labor, light denied?"
　　I fondly ask. But patience to prevent
That murmur, soon replies, "God doth not need
　　Either man's work or his own gifts; who best
　　Bear his mild yoke, they serve him best; his state
Is kingly; thousands at his bidding speed
　　And post o'er land and ocean without rest:
　　They also serve who only stand and wait."

Much is compressed into the final image of standing and waiting. The image is first of all an image of monarchy—attendants to a king or queen residing at court. Applied at a spiritual level, it is a picture of God's heavenly court. To catch the full meaning of the picture, we need to trace the Christian virtue of waiting through the Bible, where it represents such qualities as patience, resignation, dependence, contentment, hope, and joyous expectancy in anticipation of the return of Christ. The relevance of the sonnet for purposes of this book is the general movement of the poem, in which the hope and anticipation of heaven is the answer to the problem of human suffering in this life.

The same movement underlies a sonnet that Milton wrote earlier in life, perhaps as a Puritan love poem addressed to his first wife (whom he married when she was sixteen). The poem begins by picturing life as a pilgrimage up an archetypal "hill of difficulty," after which it goes on to praise a life of spiritual virtue as a preparation for heaven:

> Lady, that in the prime of earliest youth
>> Wisely hast shunned the broad way and the green,
>> And with those few art eminently seen
>> That labor up the Hill of Heavenly Truth,
> The better part with Mary and with Ruth
>> Chosen thou hast; and they that overween,
>> And at thy growing virtues fret their spleen,
>> No anger find in thee, but pity and ruth.
> Thy care is fixed and zealously attends
>> To fill thy odorous lamp with deeds of light,
>> And hope that reaps not shame. Therefore be sure
> Thou, when the Bridegroom with his feastful friends
>> Passes to bliss at the mid-hour of the night,
>> Hast gained thy entrance, virgin wise and pure.

Here is Milton's picture of the Christian life as a pilgrimage—a life of single-minded devotion to Christ in the face of criticism by people who do not share the vision.

TRACING THE TRANSCENDENT: HEAVEN IN *PARADISE LOST*

Paradise Lost is the great English epic. An epic is a long poem written in an exalted style. Reading Milton's epic is both demanding and rewarding. A good piece of initial advice is to avoid getting bogged down in parts of the poem that seem beyond a reader's capability or interest of the moment. One can always go back and read those sections later. While Books 3 and 4 are the gold mines so far as the subject of this book is concerned, it is useful to know what happens elsewhere in the story, inasmuch as glimpses of heaven pervade the entire poem.

Paradise Lost is the story of all things. It covers the history of the world, enclosed at both ends by eternity. Although Milton rearranges the chronology of his story to fit the epic convention of beginning "in the middle of things," by the time we finish his poem we have gone through the life of the world in its entirety: creation, life in Paradise, the Fall, life in a fallen world, the end of human history. Heaven is the constant factor against which these events occur, and after hell is created for the punishment of the rebellious angels, it, too, is part of the background for the human story.

Viewed most simply, the structure of Milton's story is a threefold movement, tracing the antecedents, occurrence, and consequences of the fall of Adam and Eve. The Fall itself occurs in Book 9. The story thus falls into a great division of *before* and *after* the Fall, a division that confronts the reader with a choice between good and evil, innocence and evil. The implication of the story is clear: attaining heaven means choosing one set of values and rejecting another.

Ostensibly Milton does not tell the story of a quest for heaven. Unlike the stories that Dante and Bunyan tell, *Paradise Lost* contains no pilgrim journeying from hell or earth to heaven. But in subtle and submerged ways that paradigm is present in *Paradise Lost,* as we can see if we trace the outline of the plot. Milton arranged his twelve-book epic by pairs of books, and I have followed that pattern in tracing the progress of the poem.

"CELESTIAL SPIRITS IN BONDAGE"

The first two books of *Paradise Lost* tell the story of Satan and his fallen angels in hell. These books are filled with recognizable human experience, in a demonic mode. As we listen to Satan and his cohorts talk in their first moments in hell, we actually experience such common human experiences as defiance against God, evil, self-initiated suffering, defeat, irrevocable loss, egomania, the desire for revenge, hatred, and delusion.

In a sense, then, we begin Milton's story in the same spiritual realm as Dante's Inferno or Bunyan's City of Destruction. As in those works, we are given to understand that any attainment of heaven begins at the greatest possible distance from it, in the mire of total spiritual bankruptcy. Although there is no pilgrim to represent us in Milton's story, as readers we are led to contemplate the same quest that stories of pilgrimage narrate. In this case it is the *reader* who is made aware of the need for rescue from the destruction of evil and who is led to long for the realm from which the demons have fallen.

Another subtlety at work in the first two books of Milton's story is that even though the ostensible subject is life in hell, the demons keep giving us glimpses of heaven as they discuss the terrible change that has engulfed them. In effect, they subvert the apparent plot—the heroic energy of the demons in rousing themselves from the burning lake—by opening doors and windows into the superior glory of heaven. Satan's very first speech, for example, begins as an address to Beelzebub:

> If thou beest he—but O how fall'n! how changed
> From him who in the happy realms of light
> Clothed with transcendent brightness didst outshine
> Myriads though bright.

For a moment we are lifted right out of the misery of hell into the glory of heaven. When Beelzebub replies, he makes a comment about "all our glory extinct, and happy state / Here swallowed up in endless misery," and again we are led to desire the heavenly state from which the angels fell. "Is this the region," Satan will later ask, "that we must change for heaven, this mournful gloom / For that celestial light?" Satan answers the question with a perverse, "Be it so," but the reader has quite a different assessment.

To sum up, the first two books of Milton's poem, while most obviously portraying life in hell, also contribute to Milton's heavenly vision. They establish in palpable images and characters the reality of an evil that stands opposed to heaven—an evil from whose grip Milton's readers realize they must be rescued. The atmosphere of Milton's hell is suffocating, and gurgling around in it makes the reader long for a corrective in the form of God and heaven. That longing is unwittingly fostered by the fallen angels themselves as they speak constantly of the horrible change in their situation and their wished-for reascent to the place from which they have fallen.

"THE HAPPY REALMS OF LIGHT"

Books 3 and 4 of *Paradise Lost* are Milton's vision of perfection, in heaven and in Paradise, respectively. Since these will be the focus of this chapter, I will note here only how they fit into the ongoing flow of the poem. Having awakened a longing for the antithesis of hell, Milton satisfies that longing with his pictures of life in heaven and Paradise. Life in heaven and Paradise is the reverse of what we have seen in Books 1 and 2. What the citizens of hell despise, the angels in heaven, as well as Adam and Eve in Paradise, delight to do. Hell is dark, heaven is light. Hell is self-centered, heaven and Eden are God-centered. Whereas the angels in heaven delight to praise God, one of the fallen angels in hell paints a sarcastic picture of heavenly worship (2.241–50), leading to Charles Williams's famous quip, "Hell is inaccurate."

By the time we get well into Book 3, then, it becomes obvious that Milton has portrayed the great "either-or" of existence. For every creature, whether angelic or human, the universe is conceived as a great divide between heaven and hell, goodness and evil, God and Satan. The preface to C. S. Lewis's *The Great Divorce* is one of the most helpful commentaries that one can read on *Paradise Lost*. "Blake wrote the Marriage of Heaven and Hell," comments Lewis; "I have written of their Divorce." So did Milton, agreeing with Lewis's viewpoint three centuries later that it is a fallacy to suppose that "reality never presents us with an absolutely unavoidable 'either-or.'" Reading *Paradise Lost* makes us feel what it is like to live in a universe where "every square inch, every split second, is claimed by God and counterclaimed by God" (Lewis, *Christian Reflections* 33). In short, Milton structured his vision of heaven on a dialectical principle, setting it over against its opposite.

One function of Books 3 and 4 of *Paradise Lost*, then, is to give us the second half of a great divide. The darkness of hell drops out of sight momentarily, except for the latter parts of both books, where the focus returns to Satan's journey toward earth. With the air cleared, we are free to breathe the exhilarating freshness of perfection.

"WARRING IN HEAVEN AGAINST HEAVEN'S MATCHLESS KING"

When God dispatches the angel Raphael to visit Adam and Eve and warn them of Satan's presence in the garden, the angel tells Adam the story of the war in heaven that preceded his creation. This occupies the next unit of *Paradise Lost*, Books 5 and 6. There are many pictures of heaven as a place and state of soul in these books, as there are throughout *Paradise Lost*, but I have space only to say something about the very idea of war in heaven, a thought that seems incompatible with heaven and that is largely absent from the other works of literature discussed in this book. We all know that we must travel *through* evil en route to heaven, but how can evil actually be present *in* heaven?

We should note first that Milton, as nearly always, was getting his material from the Bible, embellished by the commentary that had grown up around it during the Christian ages. The Bible tantalizes us with pictures of a great angelic war in heaven, though it does not give us many details. The main text is Revelation 12:7–12, beginning with the evocative statement, "Now war arose in heaven, Michael and his angels fighting against the dragon" (RSV). Old Testament pictures of a satanic figure expelled from heaven lend further details to this mysterious event (e.g., Ezekiel 28:11–19 and Isaiah 14:12). While these passages push the celestial war back into prehistoric eternity, other passages raise the possibility of more continuous demonic assault on heaven. When seventy of Jesus' disciples returned with news of their having cast out demons, for example, Jesus replied, "I saw Satan fall like lightning from heaven" (Luke 10:18 RSV).

We can make an interesting application of Milton's story of war in heaven to the theme of this book—the quest for the Celestial City. One of the dominant themes in the literature of pilgrimage is the account that this literature gives of the obstacles to the attainment of heaven. It so happens that the behavior of Satan during the celestial battle provides a veritable anatomy of ways to lose heaven.

In Milton's story, the war in heaven starts in an act of satanic envy of Christ when God the Father exalts His Son before the angels. Satan, Milton tells us, "could not bear / Through pride that sight, and thought himself impaired" (5.664–65). Pride leads to rebellion, as Satan gathers a third of the angelic host to his side. Lust for power and a desire for self-aggrandizement fuel Satan's three-day battle with God. Having set himself against God, Satan hardens himself in sheer hatred of God and goodness, finally preferring to reign in hell than serve in heaven (he had already made that claim in Book 1, lines 261–63).

Here, then, is one of the lessons that we can learn from Milton's epic war in heaven: heaven is not simply the realm to which the human soul aspires—it is a realm that the human race has lost. I am reminded of T. S.

Eliot's portrayal of heaven as the place at which we arrive "where we start-ed / And know the place for the first time" ("Little Gidding," lines 241–42). Milton's repeated picture throughout *Paradise Lost* is one of creaturely standing or falling. In the dialogue in heaven in Book 3, God the Father says about the angels, "Freely they stood who stood, and fell who fell" (3.102). In a similar vein, Raphael says in his lead-in to the account of the war in heaven (5.536–43),

> Myself and all th' angelic host that stand
> In sight of God enthroned, our happy state
> Hold, as you yours, while our obedience holds;
> On other surety none; freely we serve,
> Because we freely love, as in our will
> To love or not; in this we stand or fall.
> And some are fallen, to disobedience fallen,
> And so from heaven to deepst hell; O fall
> From what high state of bliss into what woe!

This is very revealing as an analysis of what causes a creature to lose or gain heaven. Obedience to the will of God and love of Him are the great qualifications for being in heaven. No one is barred from heaven by an outside force; every creature chooses to stand or fall.

The climax of the celestial battle is one of the high points of Mil-ton's story. After the good and bad angels have reached a standoff, God the Father delegates His Son to win the victory on a symbolic third day. "None but thou / Can end it," the Father tells the Son. When the Son appears in a celestial chariot, the rebellious angels are so terrified that they hurl themselves from heaven. Milton manages Christ's conquest in such a way as to make it a threefold action. Within the logic of the story, it is an account of the end of the prehistoric war in heaven at which the Bible hints. There are enough allusions to the Passion story in the Gospels to allow us to interpret it as a symbolic account of Christ's defeat of Satan by His death and resurrection. And there are enough allusions to the book of Revelation to make it clear that Milton intends it as a picture of Christ's defeat of Satan at the end of history. In all three cases, it is obvi-ous that the Messiah, God's anointed, is the one who secures heaven for creatures who place their faith in Him.

"TO CREATE IS GREATER THAN TO DESTROY"

Milton balances his story of the war in heaven with a pair of books that narrate God's creation of the world and people (Books 7 and 8). We see here the impulse to balance loss with restoration, destruction with creation, that is inherent in the Christian view of reality. While the story of creation is less obviously relevant to the theme of the search for the Celestial City than other parts of Milton's story, we should not discount it. The earthly creation appears so irresistibly wonderful in Milton's descriptions of its making that we can hardly fail to experience it as a kind of suburb of heaven. It possesses many of the qualities of heaven. The implication is one that reminds us of C. S. Lewis's theory that our best earthly moments were never intended by God to satisfy us but only to awaken our longing for something better, namely, heaven.

The climax of Milton's creation story is the creation of Adam, representative of humankind (8.249–99). Milton allows his character Adam to tell the story himself, in the form of a drama about his emerging consciousness. Adam's first act is to turn his eyes "straight toward heaven" (8.257). It may seem like an insignificant detail, but in Milton's story it is laden with meaning. Made in the image of God, Adam's implanted aspiration as a human is toward heaven.

Throughout every part of *Paradise Lost*, we get glimpses of heaven, confirming that Milton's imagination "homes" to heaven. For example, we get this account of God's leaving heaven on His journey to create the world (7.205–9):

> Heaven opened wide
> Her ever-during gates, harmonious sound
> On golden hinges moving, to let forth
> The King of Glory in his powerful Word
> And Spirit coming to create new worlds.

When God returns to heaven after His work of creation, the heavenly hosts have a Sabbath celebration to end all Sabbath celebrations (7.584–640). These images of heavenly glory may seem only tangentially related to the theme of the search for the Celestial City, but they are not. Milton's contribution to the literature of pilgrimage is to make heaven so exalted and evocative that any believing heart would want to be there. The longing of the human heart for heaven is the subtext of *Par-*

adise Lost, even when the surface narrative is dealing with matters that seem remote from it.

"HEAVEN NOW ALIENATED"

One of Milton's narrative purposes in *Paradise Lost* is to explain how people became wayfaring and warfaring pilgrims. In Milton's view, Adam and Eve before the Fall were in a dynamic state from which, if they remained obedient, they would eventually qualify for entrance into heaven (7.157–62). If the human race in some sense began with a natural right to heaven, why is gaining heaven now such an arduous task? Milton supplies a narrative answer in Books 9 and 10, which tell the story of humankind's fall from innocence and the immediate aftermath of that fall.

The story of Eve's fall is the prototypical temptation story, and Milton elaborates it at full epic scope. In keeping with the theme of the search for the Celestial City, we might profitably read the story of Eve's fall and then Adam's fall as giving us a picture of the sins that can lose heaven for us, just as it lost it for Adam and Eve. The essence of both falls is disobedience to what God had commanded, but within that umbrella Milton differentiates the two falls. Eve's fall encompasses the sins of prolonging the occasion of temptation, trying to be self-reliant, allowing herself to be deceived, indulging her appetites when abstinence was required, and allowing her emotions to be swayed by Satan's flattery. Whereas Eve falls deceived, Adam sins "against his better knowledge" (9.887). He chooses a lesser good over the love of God and indulges his selfish desires in deciding that he cannot live without Eve.

The effects of the Fall keep expanding as we read Book 10. We see notable pictures of despair, quarreling, guilt-stricken fear of God, and disappointment. What we are led to feel most poignantly is the sense of regret over what has happened. Even this is part of Milton's heavenly vision: the dissatisfactions that we feel in our fallen state are enough to make pilgrims of us, provided we know the way to follow back to heaven and perfection. Milton's strategy for making us want heaven can be expressed partly by the formula of dissatisfaction crossed with longing.

"TILL TIME STAND FIXED"

The last two books of *Paradise Lost* reenact the epic convention of the vision of future history. In Milton's story, God dispatches the angel

Michael to earth to instruct Adam and Eve in how to conduct their earth-ly life in a fallen world. The goal is to bring Adam and Eve to a state of redemption before they are expelled from the garden. In Michael's words to Adam, the purpose of the visit is "that thou may'st believe, and be con-firmed, / Ere thou from hence depart" (11.355–56).

Milton breaks with epic tradition by making the vision of future his-tory a pessimistic story of human waywardness instead of a celebration of the poet's nation. This is in keeping with Milton's strategy of showing the very real obstacles to heaven. Like Dante and Bunyan, Milton portrays in detail the conditions through which warfaring and wayfaring Christians must pick their way to the Celestial City. Also important to Milton's strategy is his portrayal of the occasional lone person of spiritual virtue (such as Noah and Abraham) who points the way for the pilgrims who follow them.

The vision of the future comes to focus on the Atonement of Christ and the consummation of history, when God will raise

> New heavens, new earth, ages of endless date
> Founded in righteousness and peace and love,
> To bring forth fruits, joy and eternal bliss.
> (12.549–51)

Adam's response to the instruction that he has received is the moment of epiphany toward which the whole poem moves, and it is Milton's moving picture of the pilgrim life that will lead a person to heaven (12.557–73):

> Greatly instructed I shall hence depart,
> Greatly in peace of thought, and have my fill
> Of knowledge, what this vessel can contain;
> Beyond which was my folly to aspire.
> Henceforth I learn that to obey is best,
> And love with fear the only God, to walk
> As in his presence, ever to observe
> His providence, and on him sole depend,
> Merciful over all his works, with good
> Still overcoming evil, and by small
> Accomplishing great things, by things deemed weak
> Subverting worldly strong and worldy wise

> By simply meek; that suffering for truth's sake
> Is fortitude to highest victory,
> And to the faithful death the gate of life;
> Taught this by his example whom I now
> Acknowledge my Redeemer ever blest.

Death is the gate to life, Adam asserts: there can be no better perspective on the quest for the Celestial City than this.

The closing lines of the poem are very moving. They portray Adam and Eve's expulsion from the garden into a fallen world. It is the famous picture of Adam and Eve's making "their solitary way" through Eden, "hand in hand, with wandering steps and slow." Milton ends his story where Bunyan and others begin it—with his human characters beginning their life as wayfaring Christians in quest for the Celestial City.

"OF THINGS INVISIBLE TO MORTAL SIGHT": MILTON'S VISION OF HEAVEN

Milton's most extended vision of heaven occurs in Book 3 of his poem. I have space only to suggest its general features. My goal will be realized if I can entice readers to read it for themselves. I will make no attempt to illustrate or prove the generalizations that I make about Milton's portrayal of heaven; my purpose is simply to provide a road map that alerts readers what to look for.

The most important thing to note is the uniqueness of Milton's story compared to other works discussed in this book. Milton is writing about heaven as it existed before redeemed people were there. This means that Milton's heaven is populated only by God and angels. Because of his story material and epic purpose, Milton is not writing about heaven as the object of human search, though indirectly the effect of his picture of heaven is to make us want to claim it as our home. As C. S. Lewis has put it, Milton's purpose is to depict "the objective pattern of things," with the result that we are invited to look at the cosmic story "from outside." Whereas Dante "is telling the story of a spiritual pilgrimage," Milton "is giving us the story of the universe itself" (*A Preface to "Paradise Lost"* 132–33).

The first thing to notice about Milton's heaven is that it is both a place and a spiritual state. Milton is sometimes criticized for making his heaven too palpable, but he had no sympathy for attempts to turn heaven into an abstraction. Milton's heaven stands foursquare at the physical and spiritual top of the universe. God sits enthroned on a mountain. We read continuously about thrones, gates, gold, a river of bliss, Elysian flowers, and celestial roses. Underlying all of these physical descriptions is the doctrine of accommodation—the principle of "likening spiritual to corporal forms / As may express them best" (5.573–74). In other words, there is an incipient symbolism at work, as Milton uses words and images to express the inexpressible.

But Milton's heaven is more than a place. It is also a spiritual state. The chief means by which Milton alerts us to this is the presence of conceptual imagery in his account—images that name qualities rather than sensory objects. Words such as "bliss," "joy," and "peace" keep coming up in Milton's descriptions of heaven. A specimen passage describes heaven as "Founded in righteousness and peace and love, / To bring forth fruits, joy and eternal bliss" (12.550–51).

Several years ago a study concluded that in modern America the view of heaven as a place to meet God has been eclipsed by a popular conception of it as a celestial family reunion (Woodward 53). By contrast, Milton's heaven is dominated by the presence and centrality of God. Here is the very first picture we get of heaven (3.56–59):

> Now had the almighty Father from above,
> From the pure empyrean where he sits
> High throned above all height, bent down his eye,
> His own works and their works at once to view.

In the lines following, all others mentioned—the angels, the Son, Adam and Eve, and Satan—are stationed in relation to God the Father. Here is the main feature of Milton's heaven in microcosm: God is the central focus of heaven. We might note in passing that the quoted lines suggest another leading feature of Milton's heaven—its transcendence. We are continuously aware as we read Milton's poem that heaven is high—physically, spiritually, and emotionally.

In keeping with Milton's making God the central feature of heaven, the heaven about which we read in *Paradise Lost* is very much a theological heaven. We no more enter heaven than we hear the Father and Son conduct a celestial dialogue (3.80–343) in which they discuss the fate of Adam and Eve on earth, ending with the Son's volunteering to go to earth to redeem the human race. The dialogue in heaven becomes an exalted drama of the authority, glory, justice, mercy, and love of God. By making God a speaking character like this, we, in effect, are led to contemplate theology, including the attributes of God, as we dwell in Milton's heaven.

Unlike writers who simply make heaven the goal of a human quest, Milton actually portrays life in heaven. The result is that we are given a fairly full account of what I will call heavenly ritual. The leading activities are worship of God, praise of God and His works, and enjoying a general spirit of celebration and well-being. In contrast to the static beatific vision at the end of Dante's *Divine Comedy* (where the saints sit in an amphitheater and gaze at God), Milton's heaven is filled with motion and activity. The angels regularly respond to the mighty acts of God with praise and worship. In some scenes they are a celestial cheering section for God; in others, a grand choir. Here, for example, is the scene after the dialogue in heaven in which the Son volunteers to undertake the redemption of the human race (3.344–52):

> No sooner had the almighty ceased, but all
> The multitude of angels with a shout
> Loud as from numbers without number, sweet
> As from blest voices, uttering joy, heaven rung
> With jubilee, and loud hosannas filled
> The eternal regions: lowly reverent
> Towards either throne they bow, and to the ground
> With solemn adoration down they cast
> Their crowns inwove with amarant and gold,
> Immortal amarant. . . .

This passage illustrates as well some of the imagery by which Milton portrays the glories of heaven. One is conceptual imagery—images naming qualities rather than sensory qualities, on the premise that if heaven transcends earthly reality, the imagery used to portray it should rise above the merely sensory. Another dominant image pattern is enameled imagery—images combining hardness of texture and brilliance of light to suggest a realm of permanence that transcends our cyclic vegetative world (with jewel imagery being the favorite among writers who portray heaven).

Even more dominant is the light imagery that suffuses Milton's heaven. In fact, Milton begins Book 3 with an exalted invocation in which he praises light for its creative and illuminating qualities, implicitly asking God to inspire him with those qualities in his writing of the poem. Milton's handling of light imagery in *Paradise Lost* so impressed the poets of the next generation that after Milton had written, the adjective "bright" replaced "good" as the most frequently used term denoting goodness in English poetry (Miles).

Finally, in keeping with the Purtians' preoccupation with cultivating good "affections" (their word for "emotions"), Milton's heaven is known partly by the desires and emotions of the angels who inhabit it. The dominant desire is to enjoy God's presence. The emotions that we are led to share as we enter into the spirit of the story include praise, beatitude (the state of being blessed), joy, obedience, and contentment. Within the logic of Milton's story, it is a fair inference that when human saints begin to arrive in this heaven, they will share these same affections.

"A HEAVEN ON EARTH": MILTON'S PARADISE

In his preface to *The Great Divorce*, C. S. Lewis, after noting that "if we accept Heaven we shall not be able to retain even the smallest and most intimate souvenirs of Hell," is led to ask, "But what . . . of earth?" His answer: "Earth, if put second to Heaven, [will turn out] to have been from the beginning a part of Heaven itself." This is an accurate account of the role of Paradise in Milton's poem. Milton's description of Paradise in Book 4 leaves us with the impression that it is the suburb of heaven. Furthermore, Milton's portrayal of life in Paradise is in effect his pattern of the pilgrim's life for all who seek heaven.

How does God intend human life to be lived? Basing our answer on Milton's picture of life in Paradise, several answers are obvious: in continuous communion with God and worship of Him; in harmony with nature; in companionship with one's fellow humans; with every human appetite (including the sexual) satisfied; with work to give life meaning; in contentment and joy; in reliance on God's perfect provision. An implied message is that if we wish to attain heaven, we should live as Adam and Eve lived before the Fall.

Of course, conditions for being a wayfaring pilgrim are different for people in a fallen world than they were for an unfallen couple living in a perfect garden. But there is something instructive here. The general tendency in the literature of pilgrimage is ascetic. We are given to understand how arduous the Christian life is, and how self-denying pilgrims must be as they avoid this thing, shun that one, and deny themselves the pleasures of life. But Jesus calls His disciples to enjoyment and pleasure as well as self-denial. The journey to heaven requires affirmation of God's gifts as well as a rejection of their perversions. Heaven itself is a place of pleasure and as such sanctifies all legitimate pleasure. Taking our cue from Milton's marvelous portrayal of life in Paradise, we can say that one of the prerequisites for attaining heaven is a creaturely delight in the gifts that God has given to console pilgrims on their earthly pilgrimage.

The most endearing quality of life in Milton's picture of Adam and Eve's life in the garden is the way in which nothing in Paradise is self-contained but opens upward to God in heaven. Everything in Adam and Eve's life reminds them of God. Here is a specimen passage, an excerpt from Adam and Eve's evening hymn (4.724–29):

> Thou also mad'st the night,
> Make omnipotent, and thou the day,
> Which we in our appointed work employed
> Have finished happy in our mutual help
> And mutual love, the crown of all our bliss
> Ordained by thee, and this delicious place. . . .

As they end the hymn, we observe that even something as commonplace as sleep reminds the couple of God, as they speak of "thy gift of sleep" (4.735). To see God in all of life is part of Milton's Puritan heritage, and it is the true sacramental vision (much more than the multiplying of ritual within a church), viewing all of life as pointing to God. Whereas the literature of pilgrimage is oriented toward *seeking* God, the vision of Milton and his fellow Puritans was a continuous *seeing* God in all of life.

"AND LIFT OUR THOUGHTS TO HEAVEN": MILTON'S TRUE THEME

In a day when secular literary criticism has lost its way, Milton's *Paradise Lost* is probed for what it says about all kinds of peripheral issues—politics, authority structures, the inability of language to communicate definite meaning, and such like. As I wrote this chapter, I was exhilarated to explore Milton's poem in keeping with what it is really about.

Paradise Lost is about heaven—its glory, its reality, its attainability, the obstacles that can keep us from it, and the possibility of bringing its qualities into earthly life. The word "heaven" appears more than four hundred times in the poem. Even though Milton chose epic as his medium, there is a sense in which his goal is the same as that of devotional writers of his day—to convince readers how miserable they are in their state of sin apart from God's salvation, and to delineate how sinners can attain heaven through the life of faith in Christ.

Although Milton does not tell the story of a protagonist's pilgrimage from earth to heaven, if we pay attention to the effect of his depictions on us, it becomes obvious that Milton's strategy is to arouse within us the desire to rise from earth to heaven. What Milton is best at as a poet is the poetry of longing—poetry that awakens our dissatisfaction with fallen reality and our longing for something better. A chief virtue of Milton's poetry is to give us lively pictures of the ultimate "something better."

WORKS CITED

Adams, Thomas. *The Works of Thomas Adams.* 3 vols. Edinburgh: James Nichol, 1861.

Arthos, John. *Dante, Michelangelo and Milton.* London: Routledge & Kegan Paul, 1963.

Baxter, Richard. *A Christian Directory.* Ligonier, Pa.: Soli Deo Gloria, 1990.

Kaufmann, U. Milo. *"The Pilgrim's Progress" and Traditions in Puritan Meditation.* New Haven: Yale Univ. Press, 1966.

Lewis, C. S. *A Preface to "Paradise Lost."* New York: Oxford Univ. Press, 1942.

———. *Christian Reflections.* Grand Rapids: Eerdmans, 1967.

———. *The Great Divorce.* New York: Macmillan, 1946.

Miles, Josephine. "From Good to Bright: A Note in Poetic History." *Publications of the Modern Language Association of America* 60 (1945): 766–74.

Milton, John. *John Milton: Complete English Poems, Of Education, Areopagitica.* Everyman's Classical Library. Edited by Gordon Campbell. London: J. M. Dent, 1991; Boston: Charles E. Tuttle, Everyman's Classical Library, 1993.

Perkins, William. *The Workes.* 3 vols. London: John Legatt, 1616.

Preston, John. *The Saint's Qualification.* London: Nicolas Bourne, 1633.
Woodward, Kenneth L. "Heaven." *Newsweek,* 27 March 1989, 52–55.

FURTHER READING

Milton's poetry is available in all sorts of editions, from inexpensive paperbacks to expensive scholarly editions. The best inexpensive scholarly edition of Milton's complete poems is the Everyman edition mentioned above, *John Milton: Complete English Poems, Of Education, Areopagitica,* edited by Gordon Campbell (London: J. M. Dent, 1991; Boston: Charles E. Tuttle, 1993).

Other paperback editions of Milton's complete works include *Milton: Poems* (Viking Penguin), *John Milton* (in the Oxford Authors Series published by Oxford University Press), and *The Portable Milton* (Viking).

Paradise Lost is printed in *Paradise Lost and Paradise Regained* (New American Library) and *John Milton: Paradise Lost* (Norton Critical Edition).

The most "user-friendly" scholarly edition with complete scholarly apparatus is *The Complete Poetical Works of John Milton,* edited by Douglas Bush (Boston: Houghton Mifflin).

Books that discuss the portrayal of heaven in *Paradise Lost* are likewise plentiful. My book, *The Apocalyptic Vision in Paradise Lost* (Ithaca, N.Y.: Cornell Univ. Press, 1970), analyzes the techniques by which Milton portrays the ideal supernatural (heaven and Paradise before the Fall).

The standard book on Milton's Christian doctrine is C. A. Patrides, *Milton and the Christian Tradition* (Oxford: Oxford Univ. Press, 1966).

The best general book on *Paradise Lost* is still C. S. Lewis, *A Preface to "Paradise Lost"* (New York: Oxford Univ. Press, 1942).

Stanley Fish, *Surprised by Sin: The Reader in "Paradise Lost"* (New York: St. Martin's, 1967), believes that Milton's purpose in his epic was the same as that of devotional writers of the day—to alert his readers to their fallen state and to educate them in the means by which they can recover from that state and attain heaven.

John R. Knott, *Milton's Pastoral Vision* (Chicago: Univ. of Chicago Press, 1971), explores Milton's portrayal of life in Paradise, also noting how Milton makes heaven and Paradise share some of the same qualities.

FIVE

IN THIS WORLD AND THE NEXT: BUNYAN'S *THE PILGRIM'S PROGRESS*

BY E. BEATRICE BATSON

John Bunyan, born the son of a tinker in the village of Elstow near Bedford, is the author of more than sixty books. Although many readers know his *Grace Abounding*, *The Life and Death of Mr Badman*, *The Holy War*, and others, his most enduring work is *The Pilgrim's Progress*, probably written during his prison term.

Prosecuted under an Elizabethan act against Nonconformists (those Christians not associated with the official Church of England), Bunyan was arrested and sent to prison for holding preaching services not authorized by the official church. Sentenced to three months, the term was extended to twelve years with a brief respite during the sixth year. During the twelve years, he preached to prisoners and wrote books for publication. Following imprisonment, Bunyan lived a very busy life as minister and writer until his death in 1688.

His famous allegory, *The Pilgrim's Progress*, is one among a few English books that has become a world classic. Published in 1678, the work became an immediate success and was for many years the work, next to the Bible, the most deeply cherished book in English-speaking homes. It went through eleven editions before his death. By the time of his death, it had also been translated into Dutch, French, and Welsh. The work has now been translated into more than seventy languages and dialects.

JOHN BUNYAN: STORYTELLER AND ALLEGORIST

Livingston Lowes calls *The Pilgrim's Progress* not far from the kingdom of great fiction. To understand this tribute is simply to recall features of Bunyan's power in storytelling: a hero with strengths and weaknesses evoking the reader's ability to empathize and identify, exciting adventures, struggles and triumphs, vivid characterizations, wonder and suspense, concreteness and mystery, depth in human experiences, moral stimulation, and a satisfying happy ending.

Perhaps the most striking feature of Bunyan's storytelling is its realism. C. S. Lewis once stated that "everything is visualized in terms of the contemporary life that Bunyan knew." Readers may observe this in the various details of the journey along which Bunyan's hero travels: muddy roads, rotten trees, a garden of flowers, singing birds, inclement weather, a barking dog, roads without signs, dark valleys, high hills—all aspects of Bunyan's "realistic plain dealing." Even the conversations along the way underscore the realism, in that travelers discuss whom and what they have met and seen. They talk of their families and backgrounds or gather information about the road ahead, and occasionally, they exchange gossipy rumor about acquaintances.

An equally significant feature of Bunyan's storytelling is vivid depiction of character. With only a few strokes, he shows the essence of personality. The closed-minded Obstinate, for example, who is sure he has nothing to learn either from people or books, says to Pliable (who indicated a desire to go on a Christian pilgrimage), "Tush . . . away with your Book." Later he pushes his intimidations further by exclaiming, "What! more fools still? Be ruled by me and go back!" With only one word, "briskness," Bunyan sums up the personality of the character, Ignorance. Simply by telling of By-ends's origins, associations, relatives, and bragging spirit, the author pinpoints up exactly who and what he is. He is from the town of Fair-speech, which is largely inhabited by relatives such as Lord Turn-about and Mr. Facing-both-ways. He also has connections with the parson, Mr. Two-tongues, and is always most zealous when religion goes in silver slippers.

Much of the language is that of seventeenth-century village life. The family of the hero, for example, is sure that he suffers from a "frenzy distemper," and the hero once depicts himself as "musing in the midst of my dumps." At another time when the hero was running ahead of his companion on the journey, he calls out to him in a colloquialism of the village with "Ho, ho, So-ho."

In observing the various features of the story, it is wise to remember that Bunyan places his story within the matrix of a dream. But dream is not a gateway to folly, but a vision of reality and revelation; it is not a lie, but rather a route to truth, particularly truth that is symbolic of the human condition in relation to the greater reality of Divine truth. Action in the dream world is timeless, but Bunyan includes a narrator who connects that world with the world of time or connects the world of his pilgrim with that of the reader.

While *The Pilgrim's Progress* is certainly successful as story, it is probably as allegory that the work has received its most widespread consideration. Bunyan thought hard on the nature of allegory, and in the rhymed preface to his most popular work, deemed it wise to write a defense of the form his work takes. He argues that his method comes from no less authorities than biblical predecessors, who appropriated images and metaphors, and among these are Old Testament authors, Christ in his parabolic teaching, and the apostles in their writings. Reminding readers (and perhaps his Christian critics) that his work unfolds truth within an imagined dream-story, he further defends his method on the premise that parables, too, are stories and are not to be despised, and that metaphors are figures that embody truth, and "Holy Writ" is full of figures and "allegories." What is at the heart of Bunyan's argument is the conviction that art is no enemy of truth. He understands that familiar words, such as wineskins, a barren fig tree, a lost sheep, and other commonplace terms, may be suggestive of reality beyond themselves and symbolize and illustrate spiritual truth.

To think of allegory, then, as a narrative that has meanings in addition to the literal or surface meaning is essential. Although Bunyan uses the term rather loosely, allegory is basically the interpretation of an extended metaphor. The story has its own appeal, various images have their significance, but allegory's major emphasis is on the ultimate meanings the entire story unfolds. Bunyan, then, thinks of allegory as the way words set forth one thing by another, primarily by a continuous metaphor, his being the metaphor of a journey. Through his selected metaphor of a journey, he unfolds the stages of his traveler's pilgrimage from the City of Destruction to the Celestial City.

In addition to the personal level, the work yields further understanding by observing the biblical level, which follows some of the major outlines of the Old and New Testaments. Bunyan, for example, links the Old Testament story of the safe journey of the Israelites with his metaphor of a journey. The pilgrim of *The Pilgrim's Progress* being set apart or "elected" to make the journey points to a theological level, and although the historical level appears less pervasive, the Vanity Fair episode suggests that the secular world of the seventeenth century based its well-being on supporting at any cost the economic systems of the era. Without tediously laboring to ferret out the various levels of allegory, readers will find an awareness of these levels an added enjoyment to their study.

It is important to remember that all the distinctive features of allegory are present in Bunyan's work. In addition to the dream framework, which we have briefly discussed, there are: the pilgrimage, personifications (figures of speech), and dialogue or "debate." Dorothy L. Sayers, convinced of Bunyan's understanding of allegory and noting how he appropriates the various features, refers to him as the "last of the English allegorists in the great tradition."

THE JOURNEY

The journey offers a strong, unifying structure, for any journey must begin, progress toward a goal, and ultimately reach an end. Bunyan purposes "to chalk out" the journey of a wandering pilgrim who desperately seeks "the everlasting prize." The journey begins at the City of Destruction, stretches out through the various difficult, as well as restful, places of the way, and reaches a gloriously climactic conclusion at the beautiful Celestial City. And that new city is kept before the pilgrim throughout all the struggles and joys along the way. The reader notices the numerous references to the goal in that the pilgrim (later called Christian) frequently remarks that he is headed for the heavenly city. He emphatically states to Apollyon, for example, "I am come from the City of Destruction, which is the place of all evil, and I am going to the city of Zion."

With swiftness, Bunyan firmly etches the beginning of the pilgrimage: A poor, ragged man standing off by himself, reading from the Bible, convinced that he is without hope of salvation, begins to cry out in anguish, "What shall I do? What shall I do to be saved?" Persuaded that the City of Destruction where he lives will soon be "burned with fire from Heaven" for its sin and corruption, his anguish intensifies. In his torment of spirit, he anxiously explains to someone called Evangelist that he wishes to leave the corrupt city and live forever in the Celestial City, but he does not know the way to get there. It is Evangelist who gives the burdened man his first directions of the "way he must go." But the pilgrimage has only begun.

The journey includes continuous hurdles: falling into the Slough of Despond, confronting Worldly-Wiseman, losing the Parchment Roll in the arbor, contending with false pilgrims, "clambering" up the Hill of Difficulty, battling the fiend Apollyon, trudging through the Valley of the Shadow, enduring persecution in Vanity Fair (where Faithful suffers torture, and dies), suffering the ridicule of Atheist, sinking into self-destructive despair in Doubting Castle, and descending into fear at the River of Death.

There is, however, another side to the journey, including interludes of contemplation, the special moment of unburdening at the Cross, periods of study and reflection (particularly in Interpreter's House), hours of relaxation, conversation, and fellowship in House Beautiful, times of quietness and peace on the Delectable Mountains where shepherds show Christian (and now companion Hopeful) the Celestial City, and moments of ecstasy in the country of Beulah, which lies in sight of the new city. But death still awaits the pilgrim and his companion, Hopeful. The River of Death—or indeed death itself—is not glossed over; it is a reality which must be faced before Christian reaches his ultimate goal. Although this final stage is a severe struggle for the pilgrim, both he and Hopeful cross the river and enter the Celestial City amid strains of heavenly music and glorious clanging of bells as the angelic host welcomes them home. The reader loses sight of the pilgrim in a blaze of light and in a pageant of heavenly glory.

With this picture of unspeakable beauty, probably most readers think the close of the book has come, but Bunyan adds a paragraph. He undoubtedly thinks that there are others on a pilgrimage who are impervious to the route the true pilgrim must take, and he must exhort them. In showing the character Ignorance being denied entrance into the new city, he once again reminds travelers that the way to heaven must include the Cross.

It must be noted that there are various ways to see how Bunyan shapes his journey. Perhaps some readers appreciate viewing the pilgrimage in broad outlines such as: from the City of Destruction to the Cross, from the Cross through the Valley of the Shadow of Death, from the Valley of the Shadow through Vanity Fair, from Vanity Fair to the Delectable Mountains, and from the Delectable Mountains to the Celestial City. Whether one views the shaping of the journey in broad outlines or by observing details, it becomes clear that Bunyan unifies his allegorical journey by keeping his central character in focus and by frequently referring to a definite goal that his character desperately wishes to reach.

PERSONIFICATION AND DIALOGUE OR "DEBATE"

In addition to the allegorical features of the dream framework and the journey, Bunyan also makes abundant use of personification and debate. Some personifications are rich; others are not particularly palatable to contemporary readers. What is essential is to see those capital-lettered words as imaginative interpretations. Consider Talkative. No reader wonders what the word itself means, but what does Bunyan do in order to create his Talkative? How does the author turn that capital-lettered word into his imagined interpretation? This loquacious man thinks his inquiring mind has no equal! He believes that one should talk of the "history and mystery of things" and of a breadth of subjects that will prove "profitable" and provide "knowledge of many things." His emphasis on learning and discussion sounds appealing—at least at first! Bunyan lets him talk on and on until his hollow words catch him in a web of contradictions from which he can extricate himself only by accusing Christian's companion, Faithful, of being some "peevish" man "not fit to be discoursed." What Bunyan does through his Talkative is to depict him as an empty talker, capable of talking pilgrim language, but lacking the qualities necessary to make the Christian pilgrimage.

Characteristic, too, of the allegory is the dialogue or "debate."

Although no less a literary critic than George Bernard Shaw praises the dialogue and speaks of the manner in which phrases and sentences go straight to the mark, it must be admitted that at times the dialogue is little more than stereotyped conversation. Also at times, Shaw's assessment is completely accurate, and Bunyan demonstrates his ability to give dialogue or "debate" a dramatic quality. When read in its context, the dialogue has a special excellence, as in Worldly-Wiseman's debate with Christian, when in only a few paragraphs Bunyan reveals Worldly-Wiseman's self-regard, his pretentious interest in making Christian free of his burden, his contempt for Evangelist's counsel, and his arrogant opinion that the pilgrim's sincerity comes from a weak intellect. But Bunyan also unfolds some telling aspects of Christian: he is simply not prepared for Wiseman's arguments, he is uncomfortable in the presence of one who appears unusually intelligent with a worldly reputation, and he lacks the spiritual maturity and wise discernment to respond on the level of Wiseman's thinking.

SOME THOUGHTS TO PONDER

In the various stages of his pilgrimage, Bunyan's pilgrim is not only symbolic of the wayfaring Christian making the journey from earth to heaven, but in his weaknesses, he shows characteristic traits of any finite human being. A glance at these traits of Christian, as well as the teeming characters whom he encounters, suggests recognizable features of numerous Christians: legalism, despondency, sordid thirst for wealth, slipping away from high moral and spiritual standards, pride, love of flattery, snobbery, smugness, unbelief, and overwhelming fear.

If at times he is the weak, groping human being, at other stages of the journey Christian is the strong, stable teacher. He teaches Pliable about heaven and clarifies for him some of its glories: a place where sorrow cannot enter, where companions include "Seraphim and Cherubins," and where all shall walk in God's presence, clothed "with immortality." But much of his teaching is on subjects of this world: he warns his fellow-traveler, Faithful, about the dangers of hypocrites (like Talkative) who know nothing of the costly price of making the Christian pilgrimage; he responds to Atheist's taunting remark (only after enduring others) that there is no such place as he "dreams of in all the world" with a wry statement, but "there is in the world to come"; he identifies By-ends, the reckless braggart of the town of Fair-speech, as a character who would care little for church or religion if it were not for its side advantages for making money and increasing his respectability; and he counsels Hopeful to avoid the Hill of Lucre, for it intensifies the love of money for its own sake. Teaching on the drastic differences between the true and false pilgrim is scattered throughout. Particularly pertinent is the questioning of Ignorance, which shows one who deliberately chooses his own route; but what finally brings destruction to Ignorance is not to be confused with the person of little faith. Christian urges Hopeful to understand that the pilgrim with little faith may indeed be a true pilgrim, even though he is hardly heroic. To expect the person of little faith to have the mettle of "great grace," however, is equal to blaming the wren for not being an ox. He is not to be highly commended for his small faith, but the compassionate Christian should remember that little faith does not debar one from being a true pilgrim. (The story of the character Little-faith shows this teaching in its context.)

What is also important to observe is the nature of evil. Both good and evil are realities; both are pervasive throughout the journey, but even the villains never appear to be literally consumed by evil. More familiar aspects of wrong and evil are present, such as hypocrisy, arrogance, pettiness, selfishness, narrow-mindedness, and love for worldly glory.

What characterizes Christian's victories are those qualities that characterize a Christian of any era: a compulsion to reach an essential goal regardless of the cost, resolute desire to gain knowledge of the Truth, and a clear understanding of the way one must go, unwillingness to be deterred by the numerous obstacles that may be on the route, keeping the goal constantly in focus, learning from wise teachers, and living in the spirit of expectancy with a lively faith, deep love, great hope, intensive study, and unceasing prayer.

THE END AND BEGINNING

This brief study is only a beginning of all a reader may derive from a serious reading of *The Pilgrim's Progress*. At the most general level, the book is a vivid reminder of the joys and struggles of a pilgrim who, though no plaster saint but a man with human limitations, sincerely wanted to reach the Celestial City. The goal ahead loomed larger than the numerous temptations and obstacles confronting him. As contemporary pilgrims move forward on their pilgrimages, Bunyan's book of a man on a journey will show them many experiences with which they can identify as well as new experiences that deepen their understanding of the route their various journeys may take. With this in mind, one understands more clearly the words of a distinguished Bunyan scholar, James Thorpe, who held that Bunyan "brought the language of prose narrative into contact with the human world," and he thought it fit to have his characters "use the speech of real men and women." Furthermore, he used discussions among these characters to depict the "inner world of the mind and feeling as well as the outer world of language and action." Thorpe added that Bunyan was "bold enough to take as his subject a central theme in the Christian tradition, the salvation of a human being, and deal with his subject in a literary form."

WORK CITED

John Bunyan. *The Pilgrim's Progress*. Edited by N. H. Keeble. The World's Classics. Oxford: Oxford Univ. Press, 1984.

FURTHER READING

The Pilgrim's Progress is so well known that numerous publishers print paperbound editions. Two excellent examples are The World's Classics edition published by Oxford University Press (1984; see above) and the Penguin edition (Harmondsworth, England). A splendid hardbound copy is the Clarendon Press edition by J. Blanton Wharey, revised (2d ed.) by Roger [Wharey] Sharrock (1960).

Scholarly studies abound. Two good overviews are Henri Talon's *John Bunyan: The Man and His Work*, translated by Mrs. Bernard Wall (Cambridge: Harvard Univ. Press, 1951; Irvine, Calif.: Reprint Services, 1988); and Roger Sharrock's *John Bunyan* (London: Hutchinson's, University Library, 1943; Westport, Conn.: Greenwood, 1984). For readers interested in the literary methods used by Bunyan, one very fine study is *"The Pilgrim's Progress" and Traditions in Puritan Meditation* (New Haven: Yale Univ. Press, 1966), by U. Milo Kaufmann. Numerous articles are easily accessible on various subjects pertaining to *The Pilgrim's Progress*. Several handbooks and guides are also available.

SIX

THE STORY OF ROBINSON CRUSOE AND THE STORIES OF SCRIPTURE

BY DANIEL E. RITCHIE

D aniel Defoe's *Life and Strange Surprizing Adventures of Robinson Crusoe* has fascinated every generation of readers since its publication in 1719. Its popularity quickly called forth a sequel, *The Farther Adventures of Robinson Crusoe* (1719), and a collection of essays, *Serious Reflections . . . of Robinson Crusoe*, published in 1720. Part of the book's popularity, especially in countries like Britain and the United States, where the cultural memory of Puritanism has been strong, comes from Crusoe's spiritual quest. For many a Christian reader, Crusoe's growing ability to understand his life through the narratives of Scripture has rung true to the interpretation of their own lives.

Daniel Defoe (1660–1731) was raised in a Presbyterian tradition whose leaders were vigorous intellectuals and writers. In Defoe's day, Presbyterians and other "Dissenters" from the Church of England were prevented from attending Oxford or Cambridge. Nor could they enter the civil service or the military. This did not prevent them, however, from establishing their own schools, like the academy at Newington Green attended by Defoe, which some consider the equal of an Oxford college. Nor did it stop them from pursuing businesses, like the successful candle-making concern of Defoe's father. Defoe himself engaged in many businesses, trading in hosiery, importing tobacco and wine, and running a brick and tile factory. He went bankrupt several times and was imprisoned both for debt and for his political journalism. Modern readers are often surprised to learn that Defoe turned to fiction quite late in life. He wrote his six major works in a single period from 1719–24 and then abandoned fiction. Defoe did not realize the literary significance of *Robinson Crusoe*, which many consider the first English novel.

Some of the most popular literature of his time included Puritan spiritual autobiographies, guidebooks for youth, and literature dealing with Providence. The power of these books lay in the encounter between theological truths (accepted as true by writer and audience) and the lives of actual human beings. To appeal to this audience, Defoe's prefaces to *Robinson Crusoe* and its sequels maintain that Crusoe was an actual man. However, Defoe's predecessor, John Bunyan, had already tapped the immense power of the fictional picture of the Christian life in *The Pilgrim's Progress*. This example provided Defoe with an uneasy way of reconciling fiction and truth when an early critic charged him with writing a mere allegory: "The Story, though Allegorical, is also Historical," he wrote. Crusoe's shipwreck, conversion, and rescue are not historically verifiable, but they realistically portray the way a person may understand the workings of Providence in his life. Although the events are fictional, they are a true picture of life.

THE PURITAN LITERARY HERITAGE OF *ROBINSON CRUSOE*

The guidebooks and spiritual autobiographies written in Defoe's day are the most important sources for this novel. However, Defoe also knew the contemporary accounts of castaways, such as Alexander Selkirk. Selkirk's famous stay of four years on a South Pacific island provided Defoe with the dramatic situation for *Robinson Crusoe*, as well as details like Crusoe's striking goatskin cap. But the shape for the novel derives from Puritan literature. The basic pattern involves the Lord's providential doings before conversion, conversion itself, recovery, decay, and the subject's present position (Starr 40). These autobiographies saw the Christian life as a single story, a narrative whole. Often they pictured it as a journey, in which the climactic moment was conversion. Not surprisingly in an age of travel and discovery like Defoe's, this journey was sometimes a sea voyage. As J. Paul Hunter has shown, these books charted the Christian's life from the setting out, through rebellion, conversion, the tempests of spiritual warfare, and a final arrival at the "Celestial Canaan." These books tried to be realistic in describing setbacks as well as triumphs. The best of them did not suggest that conversion ended every spiritual problem in life.

Although *Robinson Crusoe* itself has little to say about heaven, Defoe's earlier guide to the Christian life, *The Family Instructor* (1715), takes it for granted that the requirements for gaining a heavenly afterlife are of utmost importance to our life in this world. Defoe's concern in this book, above all, is to treat realistically both genuine repentance and the repudiation of the Christian life. Set in dialogue form, *The Family Instructor* begins with a child's worries over eternal punishment. His father explains the Gospel in rather full detail. Even here, the book concentrates less on heaven than on conversion. The child experiences genuine "converting grace," and his mother later explains that he will enjoy the life of Christ "as thou growest up." By contrast, the older siblings, like the future Robinson Crusoe, are rebellious. After much conflict, the daughter repents, and she and her husband begin to live in harmony with her parents. The oldest son, however, does not repent. After suffering the amputation of an arm due to a combat injury, he is brought to the point of repentance, but then draws back. The final dialogue of *The Family Instructor* has the rebellious son taking the opposite road from Crusoe's: refusal to acknowledge his sin against God, a dissolute life, and a delirious death, presumably followed by his damnation.

These spiritual guides and autobiographies saw every Christian's life as both unique and yet consistent with the typical stories of the Bible. The unique events of one's own life answered to the "types" (especially the plots and characters) found in biblical narratives. In Crusoe's case, the collision between his life and the biblical types produces the most striking illuminations of his sinfulness, his setbacks on the road to conversion, and later, his spiritual maturity. Ultimately, the reader could see that even the disasters of the believer's life were necessary for some providential purpose. The fears and sufferings of a Robinson Crusoe could lead to greater spiritual depth for both character and reader.

Like the autobiographers, Crusoe sees his own life story as a spiritual guide for others. Several times Crusoe remarks that his purpose is to help others recognize the providential signs of mercy and warning. Defoe's contemporary, Isaac Watts, summarized God's providential care in his hymn "I Sing the Almighty Power of God," whose last stanza is:

> Creatures as numerous as they be,
> Are subject to thy care;
> There's not a place where we can flee,
> But God is present there.

It requires the entire novel, including his first twenty-five years on the island, for Robinson Crusoe to learn the truth of this.

Many modern readers see Crusoe learning to overcome and control the environment and persons with whom he comes in contact. But the deeper challenge is for Crusoe to learn to acknowledge God. His worldly actions must reflect a mature trust in Providence in each new scene of life. The book is structured around Crusoe's growing trust in God. At each point where the narrative comes to either a lull or a point of high tension, Defoe invents a new series of incidents that push Crusoe to a higher level of trust in God.

CRUSOE'S REBELLION AND CONVERSION

Robinson Crusoe runs away to sea just before his nineteenth birthday, an act he later learns to regard as his "original sin" (141). His first sea storm fills him with thoughts of the Prodigal Son, and like the Prodigal, he resolves to "go home to [his] Father" (8). But Crusoe's mind changes with the weather, and he continues his rambling ways. Shortly afterward, a far worse storm is interpreted by Crusoe's kindly shipmaster as the "visible hand of heaven." Like Jonah, Crusoe is not meant for the sea, says the shipmaster (12–13). But Crusoe's mind changes with his fortune. At this point the stories of the Bible (Jonah, the Prodigal Son) have no personal significance for him.

After one successful voyage, Crusoe's next venture is beset with disaster. His ship is captured by pirates, and he is enslaved for two years. Crusoe's escape from slavery, while exciting, has no significance beyond enabling him to pursue economic betterment. His treatment of his companion during the escape, while kind by seventeenth-century standards, has little of the spiritual depth of his later friendship with Friday.

Crusoe settles in Brazil, where his tobacco crop begins to bring prosperity by his fourth year there. However, Crusoe is tempted to "[rise] faster than the nature of the thing admitted" (29) and enters an illegal slave-trading operation. Barely a month after he sets out for Africa, his ship is caught in a storm fatal to all but Crusoe himself. He is "sav'd, as I may say, out of the very Grave," on his birthday, September 30, 1659, and remains on an island for over twenty-eight years.

In the days following his shipwreck, Crusoe is beset by fear, which Christians in Defoe's day considered the direct opposite to trusting in Providence. Crusoe spends the first night in a tree for fear of wild beasts. He fears losing the goods that he has salvaged from the shipwreck. He makes endless fortifications at his dwelling for fear of attack by man or beast. Yet the largest animals on the island are goats, and he is unaware of any human presence for many years. It is nevertheless easy to sympathize with Crusoe: His fears of violent predators, on the one hand, or of destitution and starvation on the other, may be realistic in his case. His fears touch something analogous to that experienced in the world of many a reader.

During these days, Crusoe occasionally considers the significance of his situation. Thinking of his dangerous journey from the ship to the island and recalling Christ's cleansing of the ten lepers in Luke 17, Crusoe says, "Did not you come Eleven of you into the [Life] Boat, where are the ten?" He makes a chart comparing the good and evil of his situation, balancing them like debits and credits, and giving God the credit for saving him. He notices some barley growing, which he connects to God's miraculous care—until he remembers having thrown it carelessly on the ground. He asks for God's mercy during an earthquake. But these reflections and gestures are merely the first steps on Crusoe's pilgrimage. In the early months, his life could go in many directions other than that of trusting God.

In the eight months after the shipwreck, it becomes increasingly clear that Crusoe is going to escape starvation. But achieving relative prosperity is not the climax of the narrative. The climax comes in Crusoe's spiritual rebirth. This occurs in the ninth month, a gestation period that some readers think Defoe consciously intended. Crusoe falls deathly ill of a fever, and in this state he dreams of an angel holding a spear: "Seeing all these things have not brought thee to Repentance, now thou shalt die," says the angel (65). At this point Crusoe's conscience begins to awaken. As a first step, he is led to acknowledge God's existence and providential control over nature. He even acknowledges his own misspent life. But these are the products of Crusoe's "natural" theology. They are spiritual insights he can achieve without God's direct help. Like the spiritual auto-biographies, *Robinson Crusoe* indicates that a saving knowledge of God must come from divine revelation.

As Crusoe begins to recover, he searches through a sea chest, the proverbial repository of valued but unused belongings (Hunter 157). Crusoe finds a Bible. In between doses of his medicine, Crusoe "opened the Book casually," reading the first words he finds: "'Call on me in the Day of Trouble, and I will deliver, and thou shalt glorify me'" (69; cf. Psalm 50:15). At this point, Crusoe begins to consider the possibility that his identity is captured and explained within the narratives of Scripture:

> The Words were very apt to my Case, and made some Impression upon my Thoughts at the Time of reading them, tho' not so much as they did after-wards; for as for being deliver'd the Word had no Sound, as I may say, to me; the Thing was so remote, so impossible in my Apprehension of Things, that I began to say as the Children of Israel did, when they were promis'd Flesh to eat, Can God spread a Table in the Wilderness [Psalm 78:19]? (69)

There are three parts to the "plot" of Psalm 50:15: calling on God, being delivered, and glorifying God. As he returns to health, Crusoe can now see how God has continually delivered him. "But I had not glorify'd him," he realizes (70). During his very next Bible reading, Crusoe places himself among the audience that listens to the testimony of Peter and the apos-tles: "[Christ] is exalted a Prince and a Saviour, to give Repentance, and to give Remission" (Acts 5:31). This verse calls forth Crusoe's own prayer for repentance and enables him to understand the "deliverance" of Psalm 50 "in a different Sense from what I had ever done before" (71). That is, he seeks (and finds) deliverance from the guilt of his past life. Compared to this true, spiritual salvation, deliverance from the island would be a fig-ure or analogy.

The continued popularity of Robinson Crusoe, especially among Christian readers, rests on moments like this one, where the realism of the spiritual narrative is united with the realism of the island adventure. This unity makes Crusoe an Everyman, recapitulating in his island existence the drama common to everyone who learns to trust God.

CRUSOE'S IDENTITY AND BIBLICAL NARRATIVE

Beginning with his climactic conversion, Crusoe begins to find his world in the stories of Scripture. During the next decade he recognizes that his life is described by Psalm 78—God's Table is indeed spread in the Wilderness—as he learns to make clothes and pottery and becomes a baker and goatherd. He also comes back to Psalm 50:15 during the next crisis of his life, fourteen years later, when he discovers a human footprint on the island. This discovery is so frightening that his fears threaten to undo all the progress he has made in the spiritual life (114).

The biblical narratives provide a structure for the book, but they are short enough that many modern scholars underestimate their importance. Instead, they treat *Robinson Crusoe* as a novel about economics and survival, or they see Crusoe's religious thoughts as rationalizations for his material concerns. Yet even in the passages where these concerns are prominent, his growing understanding of Providence is usually more fundamental. During his third year on the island, for instance, Crusoe's barley and rice crops are increasing so fast that "I really wanted to build my Barns bigger," he says (90). This would enable him to plant only once a year rather than twice. This plan—which he does not carry out—alludes to the foolish man who longs for greater barns (Luke 12:16–21). The man in the parable—who never carries out his plan either—is not "rich toward God." Immediately thereafter, another plan begins to obsess Crusoe: to build an immense canoe to leave the island. The project costs him six months of fruitless labor, for Crusoe finds it impossible to move the huge craft from the construction site to the water (93). In reflecting on this, he alludes to Luke 14:28 in remarking "the Folly of beginning a Work before we count the Cost." In both of these cases, Crusoe learns how to apply the stories of the Bible to his own life. He gains temperance and prudence by reflecting on his experience through the medium of Scripture.

As the fourth anniversary of his shipwreck approaches, this most calculating of men says that his "constant Study, and serious Application of the Word of God" had produced a different Notion of Things. I look'd upon the World as a Thing remote, which I had nothing to do with . . . and well might I say, as Father Abraham to Dives, Between me and thee is a great Gulph fix'd. (93–94; cf. Luke 16:19–31)

The "world" Crusoe lived in before the shipwreck, in other words, is likened to the distant, tormenting fires of Christ's parable. On his island, by contrast, there is an immediate connection between Crusoe's plans—whether to build barns or canoes—and their true value. The connection is that of Providence. In this setting, coveting more grain or wine or timber than he can use is obviously and immediately foolish, as Crusoe comes to realize. By contrast, prudential plans and temperate consumption are rewarded.

Crusoe is now four years into his island existence, taking major steps on his spiritual journey. Although his steps are often backward as well as forward, he knows which direction is the correct one. He frequently "admire[s] the Hand of God's Providence, which had thus spread my Table in the Wilderness" (95). He is learning, through successes and follies, that his life can indeed run in the providential patterns of the psalmists and gospel writers.

The significance of Crusoe's life is not reducible to abstract virtues (such as prudence or temperance). Rather, these qualities, along with other needful ones, are discovered and developed through the events of his life. In particular, he develops a growing ability to trust in the truths of scriptural narratives as they intersect with his life story.

Defoe later tried to separate the theological truths of the book from its narrative. *The Serious Reflections* is a set of essays on Providence, honesty, solitude, and other topics, but readers have never much cared for them.

FEARS, FRIENDSHIP WITH HIS "MAN FRIDAY," AND DELIVERANCE

By his fifteenth year on the island, Crusoe appears to be leading a balanced Christian life. But he continues to long for society with other persons, and Defoe interrupts his calm life in an entirely unlooked-for way:

It happen'd one Day about Noon going toward my Boat, I was exceedingly surpriz'd with the Print of a Man's naked Foot on the Shore. . . . I stood like one Thunderstruck, or as if I had seen an Apparition. (112)

Crusoe is immediately overwhelmed with a fear of cannibals. This "Fear banish'd all my religious Hope, all that former Confidence in God which was founded upon such wonderful experience as I had had of his Goodness, now vanished . . ." (113).

As in his conversion, Crusoe looks back to Psalm 50:15 in the current crisis: "Call upon me in the Day of Trouble, and I will deliver, and thou shalt glorify me." But Crusoe finds himself unable to do this successfully. Instead, he thinks of releasing his goats and plowing under his grain, lest the savages become aware of his presence. He begins to look upon his dwelling as a "castle," which he fortifies and conceals again, as he had done in the fearful days before his conversion. In short, the incident subjects him to "the constant Snare of the Fear of Man" and prevents him from resting upon Providence (116). After two fearful years, Crusoe finally witnesses a cannibal feast on his island. This causes him to waste even more time—three years—thinking of how he might interrupt and destroy the next feast. Finally, however, he begins to ask whether he should consider himself the executioner of the cannibals. "How do I know what God himself judges in this particular Case?" he asks (124). Since God alone is the "governor of nations," he concludes, he decides to avoid intervening altogether "unless I had a more clear Call from Heaven to do it, in Defence of my own Life" (126).

Crusoe returns to a more trusting relationship with God, but his fears, now quite justifiable, prevent him from making any further advance in his outward manner of life (128).

Though Crusoe achieves relative peace regarding the cannibals, his despair over his lack of society increases to near insanity. Crusoe even considers breaking up a cannibal feast to get one or more slaves. As the happiness of Crusoe needed interrupting after his first fifteen years, so his despair in the twenty-fifth year needs interrupting now.

At the next visit of the cannibals, one of the victims escapes, running directly toward Crusoe as two of the cannibals pursue him. Crusoe kills one of the cannibals and the fugitive kills the other, leaving the fugitive free. Thus commences the relationship between Crusoe and his "man Friday," which continues for their final three years on the island. This is the first of several incidents in which Crusoe himself becomes an agent of Providence. He saves the lives of Friday and several others, one of whom is the captain of the ship that will return Crusoe to Europe.

Some modern readers have suggested that Crusoe treats Friday as little more than a slave. Defoe makes clear, however, that Friday's "conversation"—a word that would refer to their total relationship in Defoe's day—makes their years "perfectly and compleatly happy" (159). The first fifteen years charted Crusoe's growing ability to see how God had spread a Table for him in the Wilderness. The next nine had forced him to come to terms with his fear of cannibals. The final three years show Crusoe capable of bringing the blessings of Providence to others, especially in the physical and later the spiritual salvation of Friday.

As several scholars have pointed out, Friday represents the "natural man," as he was seen through the lens of the theology of John Calvin and the philosophy of Thomas Hobbes. In Friday, a natural potential for good is present, but it is eclipsed by fears and aggressive tendencies (Hunter 130; Blackburn 366). Friday's own religion includes a certain understanding of God, but it is quite faulty. The deists of Defoe's day thought that all the nations in the world would naturally develop religions in which rewards and punishments are justly awarded after death. In Friday's "natural religion," however, all persons, wicked and just, go to be with the god Benamuckee (156; see Blackburn 370–71). Friday's conversion, like Crusoe's, requires divine revelation. "[N]othing but a Revelation from Heaven" can bring knowledge of Jesus Christ's redemption to Friday (158), Crusoe realizes. With much prayer, he tells Friday the Gospel.

Friday's conversion is frankly less interesting than Crusoe's. It is not told from Friday's perspective and, therefore, readers cannot sympathize with him as they do with Crusoe. The purpose of Friday's conversion is rather to push Crusoe to greater spiritual depths. After Friday's conversion, Crusoe admires him as a "much better [Christian] than I" (159). In fact, Friday speaks of returning to his own land (along with Crusoe) to teach his people to "know God, pray God, and live new Life" (163). His questions lead Crusoe into a deeper knowledge of Scripture. This relationship, like the previous climactic incidents in the book, lead Crusoe to a new level of trust in and knowledge of God.

From this point on, Crusoe experiences few inner conflicts. The narratives of Scripture diminish in importance. The end of the novel reads more like an adventure tale with a Christian character, rather than the tale of a man whose character is being fashioned in mysterious harmony with biblical narratives. The sequels are filled with "religious" material, but they contain no clash, so crucial to the formation of Crusoe's identity, between his story and scriptural narratives.

Defoe's popularity in the eighteenth and nineteenth centuries largely rested on the realism with which his books described the spiritual struggles of ordinary people. His most popular works in 1800 were *Robinson Crusoe*, *The Family Instructor*, and *Religious Courtship*. When a significant edition of Defoe's works appeared in 1810, its editor wrote that "society is for ever indebted to the memory of De Foe, for his production of a work in which the ways of Providence are simply and pleasingly vindicated." Twenty years later, this quotation made its way into a biography of Defoe by Walter Wilson, who in turn influenced the reading of Defoe throughout the century. Of *Robinson Crusoe*, Wilson wrote:

> Whilst it instructs us in the development of the human powers, under the guidance of natural reason, it points to the Almighty as the source from whence man derives his capacities, and to whom his homage should be directed. The reader of Crusoe is taught to be a religious, whilst he is an animal being. But his lessons of this kind are no where out of place; they are closely interwoven with the story, and are so just and pertinent in themselves, that they cannot be passed over, but the attention is irresistibly rivetted to them as an essential part of the narrative. (Rogers, *Critical Heritage* 91)

As the 1800s progressed, however, critics (as opposed to common readers) began to separate the spiritual and narrative aspects of the novel. *Robinson Crusoe* came to be viewed as a book for the schoolboy, who would revel in the details of Crusoe's struggle to survive but would "reject the religious reflections, as a strange and undesirable element in a work otherwise so fascinating" (Rogers, *Critical Heritage* 130). Although the appreciation of the novel's realism remained, and although the number of editions climbed well into the hundreds by the close of the nineteenth century, elite critics often spoke of its religious purposes in patronizing tones.

A modern Christian reader is in a particularly good place to evaluate and learn from Crusoe's encounter with "Providence." Even the most appreciative critics of earlier centuries tended to isolate particular moral lessons, as if they could be detached from the novel and applied directly to the reader. The appeal of *Robinson Crusoe* is really much deeper. It serves as a model for encountering the stories of Scripture for oneself. It calls for an honest acknowledgment of the disparity between sacred stories and one's own story. Without trivializing the difficulties and imperfections of the Christian life, it provides an example of how one life slowly realigned its earthly course to follow a heavenly direction.

CONCLUSION

Robinson Crusoe remains a popular novel in part because readers have seen a true relation between his adventures and his growing identity as a Christian. Christian readers can see that Crusoe is part of a Protestant community that values, above all, the personal significance of biblical narratives. By removing Crusoe from "the world," Defoe creates a setting where God's activity seems more immediate: both hardship and ease are fraught with meaning if Crusoe can but "read" them. When Crusoe struggles for his life during the illness at his conversion, to take the most obvious example, the struggle is literally both physical and spiritual. Much of the book's pleasure and power lie in the credibility with which Crusoe learns to see the most fundamental struggles of life through the shaping narratives of Scripture. His efforts can help the modern Christian reader attain a similar level of perception for his or her own life.

WORKS CITED

Blackburn, Timothy C. "Friday's Religion: Its Nature and Importance in *Robinson Crusoe.*" *Eighteenth-Century Studies* 18, no. 3 (Spring 1985): 360–82.

Defoe, Daniel. *Robinson Crusoe: An Authoritative Text, Backgrounds and Sources, Criticism.* Edited by Michael Shinagel. 2d ed. Critical Editions. New York: Norton, 1994.

Hunter, J. Paul. *The Reluctant Pilgrim: Defoe's Emblematic Method and Quest for Form in "Robinson Crusoe."* Baltimore: Johns Hopkins Univ. Press, 1966.

Rogers, Pat. *Defoe: The Critical Heritage.* London: Routledge & Kegan Paul, 1972.

Starr, G. A. *Defoe and Spiritual Autobiography.* Princeton: Princeton Univ. Press, 1965.

FURTHER READING

The first modern, authoritative edition of Defoe's works is currently being prepared by AMS Press, under the editorship of Jim Springer Borck and others. At present, the fictional materials are available in two places:

The Novels and Selected Writings of Daniel Defoe. 14 vols. Oxford: Blackwell, 1927–28.
Romances and Narratives by Daniel Defoe. Edited by George A. Aitken. 16 vols. London, 1895–1900.

Editions of *The Life and Strange Surprizing Adventures of Robinson Crusoe* are plentiful. Many scholars use the edition prepared by J. Donald Crowley (London: Oxford Univ. Press, 1972). Other dependable editions include Viking Penguin (1966; English Library series; edited by Angus Ross) and Knopf (1992; Everyman's Library).

I have used the Norton Critical Edition in this essay (see above). It contains some of Defoe's later prefaces and accounts of contemporary shipwrecks. In addition, it presents some of the most influential recent criticism of Defoe by Ian Watt, Maximillian Novak, George Starr, J. Paul Hunter, Leopold Damrosch, Michael McKeon, and others.

Significant Biographical Studies
Backscheider, Paula. *Defoe: His Life.* Baltimore: Johns Hopkins Univ. Press, 1989.
Sutherland, James. *Defoe.* 2d edition. London: Methuen, 1950.

Studies on the Spiritual Significance of Robinson Crusoe
Blackburn, Timothy C. "Friday's Religion: Its Nature and Importance in *Robinson Crusoe.*" *Eighteenth-Century Studies* 18, no. 3 (Spring 1985): 360–82.
Hunter, J. Paul. *The Reluctant Pilgrim: Defoe's Emblematic Method and Quest for Form in "Robinson Crusoe."* Baltimore: Johns Hopkins Univ. Press, 1966.
Starr, G. A. *Defoe and Spiritual Autobiography.* Princeton: Princeton Univ. Press, 1965.

Other Significant Materials
Richetti, John. *Daniel Defoe.* Boston: Twayne, 1987.

————. *Defoe's Narratives: Situations and Structures.* Oxford: Clarendon, 1975.

Rogers, Pat. *Defoe: The Critical Heritage.* London: Routledge & Kegan Paul, 1972.

————. *Robinson Crusoe.* London: Allen & Unwin, 1979.

SEVEN

WALKING THROUGH FIRE AND SINGING OF HEAVEN: HARRIET BEECHER STOWE'S VISION OF HEAVEN

BY MANFRED SIEBALD

O f Harriet Beecher Stowe's roughly thirty novels and collections of sketches, none was as great a commercial success and none had as powerful an impact on American thinking and the course of history as *Uncle Tom's Cabin* (1852). It roused the conscience of many Northerners about the evils of slavery in the nation and prepared the way for the abolition of that "peculiar institution" in such a way that Abraham Lincoln was only mildly exaggerating when he met Mrs. Stowe for the first time and allegedly uttered his famous greeting: "So this is the little lady who made this big war!"

But then, also, no other book of hers dramatized America's religious condition and people's choice between heaven and hell more effectively. Not only did *Uncle Tom's Cabin* expose the scandalous attitude of many contemporary Christians toward slavery, it also had much to say about the *ordo salutis*, the way of salvation, as the author perceived it. It can be read as a study of the various human types who are in need of repentance and conversion, and it follows one slave's long way through tests and afflictions until he reaches his heavenly destination. Because of this theological content, the book has been called the "most seriously biblical" novel of its age (David L. Jeffrey).

Thus, *Uncle Tom's Cabin* is a book with two very different purposes and achievements. It is a propaganda novel aiming at social and political solutions in this world and, at the same time, the story of a spiritual pilgrimage to heaven. Whoever wants to do justice to the book as a whole must read it both ways and find out how Mrs. Stowe reconciled these seeming opposites. By doing so, he will also do justice to its author, whom her biographers have called, on the one hand, a *Runaway to Heaven* and, on the other hand, a *Crusader in Crinoline* and a *Woman Against Slavery*.

THEOLOGICAL AND POLITICAL STRUGGLES

Harriet Beecher Stowe's theological interests have deep biographical roots. A minister's daughter, she wrote, at the age of twelve, a theological treatise on the question "Can the immortality of the soul be proved by the light of nature?" Later, as the wife of a professor of biblical literature, she lived in the middle of the theological struggles over the legacy of New England Puritanism and, in particular, over the extent to which a repentant sinner can influence his or her salvation and the kind of evidence of salvation one may expect in one's life. Like her sister Catharine Beecher, she viewed the Puritans' strict insistence on God's sovereignty rather critically—as she expressed in her essay *Free Agency* (1837) and would later most clearly show in her novel *The Minister's Wooing* (1859). In a famous passage of that book, she attacks Dr. Hopkins, a thinly disguised version of Jonathan Edwards, the famous theologian of late Puritanism, for prescribing too exclusively the feelings accompanying conversion and thus rendering the way to heaven overly difficult:

> There is a ladder to heaven, whose base God has placed in human affections, tender instincts, symbolic feelings, sacraments of love, through which the soul rises higher and higher, refining as she goes, till she outgrows the human, and changes, as she rises, into the image of the divine. At the very top of this ladder, at the threshold of paradise, blazes dazzling and crystalline that celestial grade where the soul knows self no more, having learned, through a long experience of devotion, how blest it is to lose herself in that eternal Love and Beauty of which all earthly fairness and grandeur are but the dim type, the distant shadow. This highest step, . . . for which

this world is one long discipline, for which the soul's human education is constantly varied, for which it is now torn by sorrow, now flooded by joy . . . —this Ultima Thule of virtue had been seized upon by our sage as the all of religion. He knocked out every round of the ladder but the highest, and then, pointing to its hopeless splendor, said to the world, "Go up thither and be saved!" (579–80)

Stowe's views allowed for a more gradual process of spiritual growth and sanctification—in fact, for a kind of pilgrimage through life. On the other hand, she went along with Edwards's belief that salvation was a matter of "holy affections" and that one cannot easily explain "outward blessings," such as social status, as a sign of one's being among the elect.

However, there was still another struggle going on around and within Harriet Beecher Stowe. Part of her modification of strict Calvinism also concerned the social consequences of belief. If God completely predestines human actions, what use is it to try to abolish social wrongs like slavery? In the first half of the nineteenth century, for many Northerners the condition of the slaves called for immediate action; however, they differed substantially in their judgment about the kind and the pace of action to be taken. With the political weights in the balance between slave states and free states shifting to and fro, some churches felt that temporary solutions such as the Missouri Compromise of 1820 avoided the real issue; and when the Compromise of 1850 introduced the Fugitive Slave Law, many Christians were outraged—among them Stowe. The more fiery abolitionists—such as Theodore Weld, who unsuccessfully agitated in the theological seminary led by Stowe's father, Lyman Beecher—advocated unconditional and immediate liberation of the slaves. Others, like her father, were convinced that the solution to the problem lay in ultimately sending the African-Americans back to Africa and that this would be a lengthy and slow process. This latter position led to the formation of the "American Colonization Society," which the Beechers and also Stowe supported for a long time. Its cause is voiced very clearly in the last chapter of *Uncle Tom's Cabin*.

TWO PLOTS IN ONE BOOK

These theological and political themes can be traced in the book's two plots: the main plot, which follows the life of Uncle Tom; and another plot, which describes the escape of the Harris family to Canada. The latter, interspersed within the main plot, begins on the Shelby plantation in Kentucky where, out of financial necessity, the owner sells two slaves, Tom and little Harry, to the slave dealer Haley. Harry's mother, Eliza, and her husband, George, who lives on another plantation, decide to escape to Canada with their child. Eliza's flight north leads her across the frozen Ohio River to the houses of friendly protectors, and she and Harry are finally reunited with George, who physically fights for their liberty. They all arrive in Canada safely.

Tom, on the other hand, is separated from his family for good when his master sells him. With a number of other slaves, the trader Haley transports him south on a Mississippi steamer. During this trip he saves Evangeline, the little daughter of wealthy Augustine St. Clare, from drowning. Her father buys Tom, and the following years on St. Clare's New Orleans estate are relatively pleasant for the slave, who develops a deep human and spiritual friendship with Evangeline until her early death. When St. Clare, the benevolent master, also dies prematurely, he cannot realize his plan to free Tom, and at an auction the slave is sold again—this time to merciless Simon Legree, on whose plantation in the Red River swamps Tom finally is brutally beaten to death when he refuses to betray two fugitive fellow slaves.

As if to remind her readers that what they have been reading has been the account of a pilgrimage, the narrator summarizes this story line toward the end of the novel, just before Uncle Tom's death:

> The longest way must have its close,—the gloomiest night will wear on to a morning. An eternal, inexorable lapse of moments is ever hurrying the day of the evil to an eternal night, and the night of the just to an eternal day. We have walked with our humble friend thus far in the valley of slavery; first through flowery fields of ease and indulgence, then through heart-breaking separations from all that man holds dear. Again, we have waited with him in a sunny island, where generous hands concealed his chains with flowers; and, lastly, we have followed him when the last ray of earthly hope went out in night, and seen how, in the blackness of earthly darkness, the firmament of the unseen has blazed with stars of new and significant lustre. (475)

Tom's story is a paradoxical movement indeed: what looks like a tragic decline from blissful family life in a domestic paradise toward a sordid death at the hands of a brutal slave-owner is depicted as a move toward a final spiritual triumph. "Earthly hope" and "earthly darkness" emerge as penultimate realities, and "the unseen" as the "new and significant" one. The Harris family's story, on the other hand, rises from a state of slavery to social and political freedom, but it lacks the spiritual depth of Tom's experiences. What was heaven like for Stowe—an innerworldly condition of personal liberty and social justice, or a transcendental haven of rest for those disadvantaged on earth?

HYMNS OF HEAVEN

What heaven means in *Uncle Tom's Cabin* becomes clearest perhaps if one listens to the hymns and spirituals that Tom sings to Eva, to the other slaves, and to himself—a part of the novel that has received little attention among scholars so far. It may be that, instead of trying to extract the outlines of Stowe's vision of heaven from the sobs of the narrator and the sentimentality of much of the plot, it is more fruitful to concentrate on the songs, which contain many traditional Christian doctrines about this life and the life to come. Not only do we encounter the anonymous revival hymns and spiritual folk songs that floated around in camp meetings of the early nineteenth century and may be said to characterize the enthusiastic piety of rural and urban revivals, but also we discover many of the great hymn writers popular at the time: Watts, Wesley, Toplady, Newton, and others. By including their theological tenets and their poetic descriptions of heaven, Stowe wove a tapestry of references against which the earthly life of her characters gains eternal contours. Looking at these songs, of course, also means to look beyond the stanzas that Stowe carefully chose and quoted, i.e., at those which she omitted but could count upon as known to her readership. Thus, we can realize what the novel's original readers also heard when listening to Tom's singing.

It is not accidental that Stowe should have made such ample use of hymns in this novel and in others. She was so well-versed in hymns that, after writing *Uncle Tom's Cabin*, she was asked to help her brother Henry Ward Beecher in assembling *The Plymouth Collection of Hymns and Tunes; For the Use of Christian Congregations* (1855), a work which, partly because of its appeal to feeling, and partly because of its inclusion of nonevangelical authors, met with a rather mixed reception. Of its 1,374 hymns, more than one hundred deal with heaven.

During the public discussion going on in the New York weekly *Inde-*

pendent in 1855 about her brother's collection, Stowe wrote a "Letter from Andover," a book review in which she summarized what hymns meant to her:

> To us, nothing is so much like heaven—so near an approach to the spirits of the just made perfect as a book of hymns. The highest feelings of highest moments are here crystallized. They are like voices from the invisible cloud of witnesses that ever surround us. They give us sympathy; we say to ourselves: These have been where we now are, have felt as we feel, and our heart revives as if a brother had spoken to us. Many of them come to us embalmed in fragrance, breathing the memory of friends who wore them in their hearts and spoke them with dying lips.

It may be for these reasons that she conveyed so many of her thoughts about heaven through the hymns of *Uncle Tom's Cabin*.

CONVERSION IS THE BEGINNING

When, during "An Evening in Uncle Tom's Cabin" (chapter 4), Mose, the clownish black boy, mimics old Uncle Peter's singing "Come saints and sinners, hear me tell," he intones one of the most popular spiritual songs of early America. The lines are taken from the folk ballad "Heavenly Union" by Elkanah Dare (1782–1826), describing how Christ saves the soul "from a burning hell," brings it "with him to dwell," and gives the singer "heav'nly union." Despite the folksy tone of the rest of the stanzas and the jocular context, the song as sung by Mose sounds the theme of conversion that runs through the novel. Wherever he goes, Tom preaches the need of becoming a Christian to fellow slaves like Prue (chapter 18) and Cassy (chapter 34), but also to his owners: "'If Mas'r would only pray!'" he tells Augustine St. Clare (chapter 27). Eventually, it is through his humble and yet firm insistence that Augustine St. Clare in his dying hour returns home spiritually (chapter 28). Eva St. Clare, whom one chapter heading calls "The Little Evangelist" (chapter 25), calls on the ne'er-do-well slave girl Topsy to have faith in Christ: "You can go to Heaven at last, and be an angel forever, just as much as if you were white. Only think of it, Topsy!—you can be one of those spirits bright, Uncle Tom sings about" (331).

That all spiritual life and all hope for heaven depends on a first experience of divine grace is emphasized even when Tom sings his last songs.

After he has emerged from his final "dread soul crisis," having successfully resisted Legree's temptation to abandon his faith, he no longer feels "hunger, cold, degradation, disappointment, wretchedness" (456). He sings three stanzas of "Amazing Grace" by John Newton (1725–1807), a hymn "which he had often sung in happier days, but never with such feeling as now." Appropriate to the occasion, Stowe makes Tom select the stanzas that speak of the ultimate dissolution of the earth and of all mortal life. This foreshadowing of his own impending death includes the hope for ten thousand years and more in which to sing God's praise. However, the song is usually sung as a celebration of the grace received in conversion; it moves from a description of the sinful state of the soul to an account of the "many dangers, toils, and snares" of the pilgrimage, and ends by looking out at God's promise of a "life of joy and peace" in His presence. The strength of Tom's patience and his quiet witnessing are so convincing that even his last tormentors Sambo and Quimbo begin to pray and are converted (chapter 40).

SPIRITUAL WARFARE

But receiving grace is only the beginning of a way which is sometimes long and arduous. Toward the beginning of the novel, during a "meetin'" in Uncle Tom's cabin on Shelby Farm, the congregation sings not only "the well-known and common hymns sung in the churches about," but also those "of a wilder, more indefinite character, picked up at camp-meetings," such as

> "Die on the field of battle,
> Die on the field of battle,
> Glory in my soul."
> (41–42)

Without the singers realizing it at the time, this song, with its popular military imagery, foreshadows Tom's fate at the end of his journey south. However, until he can say with the apostle Paul the words of 1 Corinthians 15:57 ("Thanks be to God, who giveth us the victory") that serve as a motto to chapter 38, he has to fight a number of spiritual battles.

These battles against doubts, fears, and feelings of hate and despair sometimes seem to be too hard to fight for Tom, but again and again he is comforted and strengthened by the promise of God's invisible presence and support. After arriving on Legree's plantation, he dreams that Eva reads to him from Isaiah 43:2–3: "When thou passest through the waters, I will be with thee, and the rivers they shall not overflow thee; when thou walkest through the fire, thou shalt not be burned, neither shall the flame kindle upon thee; for I am the Lord thy God, the Holy One of Israel, thy Saviour" (406).

Another one of what Legree calls the "cursed Methodist hymns" is Isaac Watts's (1674–1748) "When I Can Read My Title Clear," of which Tom sings three stanzas shortly before his final ordeal, for example,

"Should earth against my soul engage,
And hellish darts be hurled,
Then I can smile at Satan's rage,
And face a frowning world."

(458)

The next stanza Tom sings asserts that the "wild deluge" of cares and the "storms of sorrow" will not be able to keep the believer from safely reaching his home. Before the slave can sing the final stanza about the "seas of heavenly rest," however, Legree is so enraged by Tom's evident happiness that he whips him—with the awareness that he has lost his power over him. Tom's victory consists in having fought the battle against hate and in succeeding to "love such enemies" as Legree, though it "isn't in flesh and blood" (462).

HEAVEN AS CANAAN

In the prayer meeting on the Shelby plantation, the slaves sing folk hymns about "beck'ning angels" and the "golden city," and some of the songs make "incessant mention of 'Jordan's banks,' and 'Canaan's fields,' and the 'New Jerusalem'" (42; see also 218 and 304). Some of the singers "laughed, and some cried, and some clapped hands, or shook hands rejoicingly with each other, as if they had fairly gained the other side of the river" (42). An old woman, giving her testimony, says she is waiting for death, "jest a waitin' for the stage to come along and take me home; sometimes, in the night, I think I hear the wheels a rattlin'"—an allusion to the chariot that took Elijah into heaven (2 Kings 2:11). The congregation responds by singing a folk hymn based on a poem by Watts that equates Canaan with heaven and the river Jordan with death:

"O Canaan, bright Canaan,
I'm bound for the land of Canaan."
(42)

When, soon after this, Mrs. Shelby asks for her maid Eliza, she is told by the slave boy Sam: "'Wal, she's clar 'cross Jordan. As a body may say, in the land o' Canaan." And she almost faints because at the moment she does not realize that the metaphor has a second meaning—that of Canaan as the land of freedom. This meaning is evoked by the narrator when the fleeing Eliza glances at the Ohio River, "which lay, like Jordan, between her and the Canaan of liberty on the other side" (68).

The songs' frequent use of Old Testament material must be seen in the light of the typological reading of Scripture that the Puritans took over from the church fathers. In much the same way as the Puritans considered their religious persecution in England to be a parallel to the biblical Israel's bondage in Egypt, the slaves referred to their own state of captivity as an Egyptian exile or a desert journey. For them, crossing the Jordan into Canaan was both an emblem of their spiritual transition to heaven and of their earthly hope for personal liberty. Such typology—as the reading of Old Testament persons, places, and events ("types") in view of their New Testament reenactments ("anti-types") is called—was frequently extended to include parallels to the respective present times of Christian believers. It forms the central theological argument of many Christian hymns and can be perceived in many spirituals. When Susan and Emmeline, Tom's fellow slaves, spend the night singing before the slave auction parts them forever, their song, "a wild and melancholy dirge, common as a funeral hymn among the slaves," draws typological parallels between their own situation and those of "Weeping Mary" and Paul and Silas (385).

The Old Testament custom of declaring every fiftieth year a year of Jubilee included the freeing of indentured servants (Leviticus 25:10)— an act that has traditionally been seen as symbolic of Christ's freeing mankind from the bondage of sin. This is the message of Augustus Toplady's (1740–78) hymn that the slaves on the Shelby plantation sing when, finally, young George Shelby has freed them:

"The year of Jubilee is come,—
Return, ye ransomed sinners, home."
(509)

Here, the novel restores the original practical meaning of an Old Testament commandment—another instance of how closely spiritual and worldly realities are connected in Stowe's view.

ABSENCE OF SUFFERING

According to critic Josephine Donovan, the songs in *Uncle Tom's Cabin* illuminate the author's utopian vision, and, as "projections of a fulfilled afterlife," they "comment dialectically on the downtrodden life the slaves were enduring." Indeed, it is hardly surprising that the one feature of heaven that Stowe uses most effectively as a contrast to the sordid realities of slavery is the absence of every suffering.

Similarly, the stanzas from comforting hymns by Thomas Moore and William Cullen Bryant which are used as mottoes for chapters 26 and 40 place dying and suffering in the greater context of earthly hope for heavenly joy. The deaths of Eva and Tom may be undeserved and terrible in the eyes of the people surrounding them and cause them emotional suffering; yet the expectation is that "heaven's long years of bliss shall pay / For all his children suffer here" (475).

The very last hymn from which the dying Tom quotes (because he is too weak to sing; the lines are "Jesus can make a dying bed / Feel soft as downy pillows are") is Isaac Watts's "Why Should We Start and Fear to Die?" The stanzas preceding the one quoted describe the ceasing of even the pains of death in heaven:

> Why should we start and fear to die?
> What timorous worms we mortals are!
> Death is the gate of endless joy,
> And yet we dread to enter there.
>
> The pains, the groans, and dying strife,
> Fright our approaching souls away;
> We still shrink back again to life,
> Fond of our prison and our clay.

In this state of being torn between life and death, the thought of eternal life without suffering induces Tom to die content and in dignity.

FAMILY REUNION IN HEAVEN

For Stowe, one of the greatest sufferings brought about by slavery was
the separation of families, and *Uncle Tom's Cabin* is full of such instances,
the first ones being Tom's being sold south and the similar fate awaiting
Harry. When Eliza escapes with her son, she dreads the separation from
her husband and voices the one hope that slaves held: she wants him to
be "as good as he can, and try and meet me in the kingdom of heaven"
(55f.). Among the whites, the "Reunion" of St. Clare and his daughter
in death (chapter 28) illustrates the same point.

Of course, in a community of Christians such a restoration of old
ties goes beyond race boundaries—as Eva expresses shortly before her
death, when talking to the slaves of the household: "'O, I am so happy,
Uncle Tom, to think I shall see you in heaven,—for I am sure I shall; and
Mammy,—dear good, kind Mammy!' she said, fondly throwing her arms
round her old nurse,—'I know you'll be there, too'" (339).

When, later, Tom and the other newly purchased slaves follow Legree
to the "dark places" of his plantation, their weary steps bear them "further from all that man loves and prays for" (398). In the song which Tom
chooses on this occasion and of which he sings his own version, his new
master senses the slave's "infernal old Methodism":

> "Jerusalem, my happy home,
> Name ever dear to me!
> When shall my sorrows have an end,
> Thy joys when shall—"
> (399)

Tom's choice is very appropriate to the situation, for if Legree had not
interrupted him, he would have gone on to sing:

> But O, the happy, happy place,
> The place where Jesus reigns;
> The place where Christians all shall meet,
> Never to part again.

The "Results" of the novel (chapter 43) show that the unity of fami-

lies can be restored even here on earth—in the earthly "Canaan" of a free
and equal society, where sisters find their brothers, and mothers their
daughters. Thus, liberty from slavery is seen to be a foretaste of heaven.

THE INVISIBLE PRESENCE OF HEAVEN

Though the old slave woman in the initial prayer meeting insists:
"Dat ar glory is a mighty thing! It's a mighty thing, chil'en,—you don'no
nothing about it," heaven is nothing distant. In a believer's eyes, reality
becomes a transparency through which heavenly things can be seen. When
Eva reads out for Tom the fifteenth chapter of St. John's Revelation, she
sees the sea of glass and the gates of pearl in the sunset around them.
Tom first sings to Eva a stanza from a spiritual folk song entitled "Wings
of the Morning," and then a part of the third stanza of Charles Wesley's
(1708–88) "And Let This Feeble Body Fail." These lines strike the note
that Eva will repeat until her premature death:

> I see a band of spirits bright
> That taste the glories there;
> They all are robed in spotless white,
> And conquering palms they bear.
>
> (304)

To Eva, heaven is tangible here on earth—she has seen the "spirits bright"
in her dreams (304). And to Tom, Eva becomes one of these spirits soon
after her death. In several dreams she appears to him in the shape of an
angel, and the narrator goes even further: "It is as if heaven had an especial band of angels, whose office it was to sojourn for a season here, and
endear to them the wayward human heart, that they might bear it upward
with them in their homeward flight" (307).

Something must be said at this point about the death of Little Eva.
Her entrance into glory has often been called unbearably sentimental.
However, a good deal of this criticism is actually aimed at the distortion
of the incident that was produced by innumerable performances of the
various dramatic versions of the novel. Hundreds of troupes produced
the play upward of a million times, thus making it the most popular
American drama of all times. And from the very first dramatization (by
George L. Aiken), Little Eva's ascent into glory proved to be just what the
audience wanted to see. Through amazing technological efforts she was

bodily lifted through the ceiling. Of course, all this glossed the scene over with an air of incredibility that did more harm to Stowe's intentions than it helped to convey her meaning. For this reason, she wrote her own dramatization, *The Christian Slave*, which was read by only one actor in a kind of lecture.

JUDGMENT

The last statement about heaven to be found in the conversations, the narrative parts, and the hymns of *Uncle Tom's Cabin* is that there is a Judgment Day waiting for everyone. This becomes obvious in Augustine St. Clare's fondness of the medieval hymn "Dies Irae" (363–64) and also in the "hymn common among the slaves" that scares Legree on his plantation:

> "O, there'll be mourning, mourning, mourning,
> O, there'll be mourning, at the judgment-seat of Christ!"
> (435)

The slave-traders and slaveholders will "go to torment," as the slaves believe, and will have to answer for their actions, as Tom's wife Chloe says with reference to the book of "Ravelations": "Souls callin' under the altar! and a callin' on the Lord for vengeance on sich!—and by and by the Lord he'll hear 'em—so he will!" (72). The importance of the book of Revelation for the novel is so obvious that it does not need to be demonstrated in detail.

Critics of *Uncle Tom's Cabin* have complained that—as Joshua D. Bellin puts it—"judgment supplants deeds as the novel's primary medium of interaction with the world." Indeed Tom, with his reliance on justice being ultimately administered by God, leaves a stronger impression on the reader's mind than does George Harris, the fiery activist. But it remains to be seen whether it is not exactly Tom's suffering that gave the novel its reformative power.

Judgment, of course, is not necessarily bad news—at least not for the believer. Significantly, St. Clare, on his deathbed, repeats only those parts of the "Dies Irae" that implore Jesus to seek and keep the sinner's soul— "words of entreaty addressed to Infinite Piety" (370). And after that he confesses that his soul has finally returned home.

PILGRIMAGE AND SOCIAL REFORM

How was Harriet Beecher Stowe able to bridge the gap between her two plots and strategies, between the theme of spiritual pilgrimage and her fight against slavery? For one thing, she stressed the biblical teaching of a last judgment in which justice will be restored and in which one's actions on earth will be weighed. In view of this judgment, the system of slavery directly affected the salvation of human beings.

To Stowe, one of the most objectionable evils of slavery was that it deprived the slaves of the Gospel. She did not show them as lacking their civil liberties alone, but as lost spiritually if they were not taught the Gospel, as Augustine St. Clare makes clear when he says of his slave that he will "have such chance of getting to heaven, at last, as I find convenient" (261).

Then, also, the "Day of Wrath" is one of which not only active evil-doers like Haley and Legree must be afraid, but also all those who could have done good and left it undone, as Augustine St. Clare realizes shortly before his death: "One should have expected some terrible enormities charged to those who are excluded from Heaven, as the reason; but no,— they are condemned for not doing positive good, as if that included every possible harm" (364). Of course, this is one of the messages of Matthew 25, a chapter in which Christ states that He will be present on earth in those who need help and that "inasmuch as ye did it not to one of the least of these, ye did it not to me." This is one of the most effective arguments of the novel for charity and social reform—one that directly connects worldly realities with heavenly ones.

The novel's insistence that ultimately it will be through God's final judgment that the wrongs of slavery are mended has been bemoaned by many critics as being a flight from reality. They would have liked Tom to be more manly and to fight out the spiritual battle with Legree physically. But if *Uncle Tom's Cabin* is so otherworldly, what explains the profound social and political impact the novel had? It seems that such critics have largely misunderstood the nature of propaganda literature. Through establishing a political or ethical tension, it creates feelings of fear and hate in its readers; but since it does not resolve this tension within the novel, the readers have to act out their moral indignation and their emotions in the real world. Therefore, it may be said that for the reading public the worldly defeat of Uncle Tom was a far more effective call to action than a physical victory would have been.

Positively speaking, Harriet Beecher Stowe saw the fight against slavery as a natural part of the Christian belief and of the hope for heaven, and she makes a very effective move in putting this conviction into the mouth of a slaveholder. Shortly before his death, Augustine St. Clare seems to summarize the practical consequences of Christianity in the middle of the nineteenth century as *Uncle Tom's Cabin* demands them from all those whites who professed to be pilgrims on their way to heaven: "My view of Christianity is such . . . that I think no man can consistently profess it without throwing the whole weight of his being against this monstrous system of injustice that lies at the foundation of all our society; and, if need be, sacrificing himself in the battle" (365).

WORK CITED

Stowe, Harriet Beecher. *Three Novels: Uncle Tom's Cabin or, Life among the Lowly; The Minister's Wooing; Oldtown Folks.* New York: Library of America, 1982.

FURTHER READING

Editions of Uncle Tom's Cabin
Stowe, Harriet Beecher. *Uncle Tom's Cabin, or, Life among the Lowly.* Edited by Kenneth S. Lynn. Cambridge, Mass: Harvard Univ. Press, 1962.
————. *Uncle Tom's Cabin, or, Life among the Lowly.* Edited by John A. Woods. London: Oxford Univ. Press, 1965.
————. *Uncle Tom's Cabin, or, Life among the Lowly.* Edited by Howard Mumford Jones. Columbus, Ohio: Merrill, 1969.
————. *Uncle Tom's Cabin, or, Life among the Lowly.* Edited by Ann Douglas. Harmondsworth, England: Penguin, 1981.
————. *Three Novels: Uncle Tom's Cabin, or, Life among the Lowly; The Minister's Wooing; Oldtown Folks.* New York: Library of America, 1982.
————. "Letter from Andover." *The Independent,* 1 November 1855, 345.

Books and Articles About Uncle Tom's Cabin
Bellin, Joshua D. "Up to Heaven's Gate, Down in Earth's Dust: The Politics of Judgment in *Uncle Tom's Cabin.*" *American Literature* 65, no. 2 (1993): 275–95.
Boreham, F. W. *The Gospel of "Uncle Tom's Cabin."* London: Epworth, 1956.

Donovan, Josephine. *"Uncle Tom's Cabin": Evil, Affliction, and Redemptive Love.* Twayne's Masterwork Series 63. Boston: Twayne, 1991.

Foster, Charles H. *The Rungless Ladder: Harriet Beecher Stowe and New England Puritanism.* Durham, N.C.: Univ. of North Carolina Press, 1954.

Hovet, Theodore R. "Modernization and the American Fall into Slavery in Uncle Tom's Cabin." *New England Quarterly* 54 (1981): 499–518.

Johnston, Johanna. *Runaway to Heaven: The Story of Harriet Beecher Stowe.* Garden City, N.Y.: Doubleday, 1963.

Joswick, Thomas P. "'The Crown Without the Conflict': Religious Values and Moral Reasoning in *Uncle Tom's Cabin*." *Criticism* 31, no. 4 (1989): 383–400.

Kirkham, E. Bruce. *The Building of "Uncle Tom's Cabin."* Knoxville: Univ. of Tennessee Press, 1977.

MacFarlane, Lisa Watt. "'If Ever I Get to Where I Can': The Competing Rhetorics of Social Reform in *Uncle Tom's Cabin*." *American Transcendental Quarterly* 4, no. 2 (1990): 135–47.

Siebald, Manfred. "The Christian Slave: Harriet Beecher Stowe's Dramatisierung von *Uncle Tom's Cabin*." *Amerikanisierung des Dramas und Dramatisierung Amerikas.* Edited by Manfred Siebald and Horst Immel. Frankfurt/Main: Lang, 1985: 55–71.

Wilson, Gayle Edward. "'As Bunyan Says': Bunyan's Influence on *Uncle Tom's Cabin.* *American Transcendental Quarterly* 1, no. 2 (1987): 157–62.

Traditional Hymns
Beecher, Henry Ward, comp. *The Plymouth Collection of Hymns and Tunes; for the Use of Christian Congregations.* New York: A. S. Barnes, 1855.

Spirituals and Revival Hymns
Jackson, Georg Pullen. *Spiritual Folk-Songs of Early America.* Gloucester, Mass.: Peter Smith, 1975.

General Background
Jeffrey, David Lyle. "Literature and the Bible: North American Literature." *Oxford Companion to the Bible.* Edited by Bruce M. Metzger and Michael D. Coogan. Oxford: Oxford Univ. Press, 1993.

Reynolds, David S. *Faith in Fiction: The Emergence of Religious Literature in America.* Cambridge, Mass.: Harvard Univ. Press, 1981.

EIGHT

A GREAT GOOD IS COMING:
GEORGE MACDONALD'S
PHANTASTES AND LILITH

BY ROLLAND HEIN

· ·

R eaders unfamiliar with the writings of George MacDonald are well-advised to begin with his fantasies for adolescents, such as *The Princess and the Goblin, The Princess and Curdie,* and *At the Back of the North Wind;* or with some of his fairy tales, of which *The Golden Key* is his finest. The style is simple and engaging, the narratives move quickly, and the adult mind cannot but be fascinated with how deftly the symbolic levels of these stories explore profound aspects of Christian life and experience.

In *The Princess and the Goblin,* the princess Irene, living in a castle, has strange and wonderful meetings with her great-great grandmother, who lives mysteriously in the uppermost room, while far underground, posing a large threat to her well-being, lives a colony of goblins. The castle becomes a metaphor for the human mind, with the mysterious possibility on the one hand of meeting the Spirit of God, and on the other, of being invaded by the dark underside of our beings, the baseness of which all people are capable.

In *The Princess and Curdie,* MacDonald intriguingly examines how spiritual growth or deterioration is related to the concept of the nature and character of God that each person holds; people react to God according to their view of what He is like. The theme of the importance of child-like faith in the ultimate goodness of God in all His acts is compellingly affirmed in *At the Back of the North Wind;* and in *The Golden Key* the author presents in the story of Mossy and Tangle moving through Fairyland a sweeping symbolic picture of the nature of the Christian life from the time of their entering it to their rising into heaven at the end.

MacDonald preferred to write such fantasies, but during his lifetime, which encompassed the last half of the nineteenth century, the novel was exceedingly popular. Writers such as Charles Dickens and George Eliot were widely read. When MacDonald discovered that he could attract a very large audience by writing novels, he began using his talent for story-telling in that form. Over his lifetime he wrote over two dozen (the exact number depends on whether one includes those written for adolescents), in which he compellingly brings to bear upon the characters his sage and penetrating insights into the Christian life.[1] These novels not only present edifying stories, but they also invite the reader to think deeply and provocatively upon what it means to live for Jesus Christ. MacDonald's gift is to define in his characters the nature of true goodness and to reveal its beauty; his writings are unexcelled in their ability to inspire one to pursue the genuinely virtuous life.

George MacDonald began his fiction-writing career with a fairy tale written for adults, *Phantastes,* and at its climax wrote a second, *Lilith,* which he intended to be his masterpiece. These are the most profound and challenging of his works, but perhaps also the most rewarding. Certainly readers who fall deeply in love with this author, as many do, become intensely curious concerning them and, at the same time, find them difficult and enigmatic. Their symbolism probes theological realities, not in any dogmatic way, but with the spirit of earnest and open exploration. MacDonald is not a proselytizer on behalf of any sectarian theology. He is a writer deeply and profoundly in love with Christ who insists that nothing in life is more important than the individual Christian's utter obedience to the Lord's teaching as contained in the Bible, and that every event that befalls a person, if it is rightly received, can be a vehicle of grace.

MacDonald was raised in a godly Scottish Calvinist home where he learned a high regard to Scripture, a love that characterized his entire life. An ideal relationship with his father greatly enriched his life as a child— his mother died when he was eight—and did much to shape his thinking as an adult. The God who invites people to know Him as a Father means for people to understand Him as the ideal Father, not as a tyrant upon a throne consumed with self-importance. As a young man MacDonald began to feel that certain discrepancies existed between the appealing spirit he found in the Bible and that of the dogmatic theology he knew. His love of the Bible, his conviction that the love of God is extended to all people, his fascination with goodness, and his confidence that only the righteous life is worth living all led him to transcend sectarian differences and become a champion for individuals to dedicate themselves to follow Christ as He presents Himself in the Gospels.

His writings all portray life as a spiritual struggle to win the prize of life in the Celestial City. *Phantastes* and *Lilith* fit nicely together to give a full imaginative depiction of the experiences that make for a spiritually successful life here and hereafter. Neither is written as a Christian tract and must not be approached as though it were. MacDonald carefully avoids Christian clichés; his intention is to explore the life of the spirit in fresh language and imagery, provoking the reader carefully to confront and think through its essential issues. Central to both works is the insistence on the new birth, which is at its heart a dying into life, a willing rejection of one's old nature in order to receive a new.

PHANTASTES

Anodos, the protagonist in *Phantastes,* awakes one morning to have the world of his bedroom begin to change into another order of reality, and a tiny woman figure invites him into Fairyland. His attitudes and responses to her suggest his low spiritual state, but his desire is intensely toward Faerie. This yearning, which C. S. Lewis is later to call *Sehnsucht* and enlarge upon in his apologetics, often motivates MacDonald's characters who are potential saints.

Faerie in MacDonald's writings is a symbol for the world of spiritual realities, both good and evil. When Anodos, whose name in the Greek can mean both "having no way" and "rising," discovers he has sufficient fairy nature to discern the dimensions of life in this higher realm, he enters to find it is as well a realm of mystery, confusion, and frightening dangers.

In it he constantly makes misjudgments and mistakes and, in spite of his best intentions, falls into the clutches of evil.

Not yet having learned that the resources of the self are insufficient for a victorious life in Faerie, his failures continue and his frustrations increase. Falling in love with a marble lady—his sense of the ideal and the perfect, for which he feels deep attraction—he soon mistakes her for another, pursues a substitute, and falls into sensuality. Further, he is plagued by his shadow—the prideful spirit of rational analysis and cynicism—that quickly destroys the glorious mysteries of Faerie with depressingly commonplace views and explanations. He is, however, helpless to dismiss it. His blunders and frustrations increase until, in the Wasteland of despair, he determines to die. Plunging into the sea, he is reborn. The scene, which is pivotal to the entire narrative, depicts imaginatively the dying into life upon which the Bible constantly insists (cf. John 12:2–25; Galatians 2:20; 5:24; Colossians 3:3).

The experience transforms his life and spirit, changing his perceptions of Faerie and his ability to live successfully and work effectively in it. The many experiences he now has present challenges and struggles for him, and he is not past the danger of failing, but he now has an inner strength, discernment, and courage that enable him to triumph. For instance, he now humbly defers to the knight, whom he recognizes as being superior to him. He now experiences a consuming, outgoing love, free from the need to be loved in return. He summarizes in chapter 24 the spiritual lessons he has learned, attitudes essential to the triumphant experiencing of Christian life.

There is much in *Phantastes* that is enigmatic and difficult to interpret. It stands in contrast to *The Pilgrim's Progress* in that, while Bunyan is concerned imaginatively to present his view of the triumphant spiritual life in more general and typical terms, MacDonald includes a considerable number of more private and autobiographical allusions. At the time of writing he was a struggling young writer with an energetic imagination and an artistic temperament. Some of Anodos's adventures, therefore, such as those that take place in the Faerie Palace and those in the Wise Woman's cottage, have as their primary reference spiritual issues and struggles MacDonald himself was facing at the time he was writing.

Further, MacDonald insists his fantasies are symbolic, not allegorical; that is, they are calculated to suggest more private and elusive meanings rather than, as in most allegories, meanings that can be fairly satisfyingly reduced to more general and explicit meanings. He suggests in his essay "The Fantastic Imagination" (Hein 423–28)—one that should be consulted by everyone interested in MacDonald's fantasy writings—that a good fairy tale should affect the reader as does a sonata, conveying one meaning to one person and perhaps another to another. To the objection "But a man may then imagine in your work what he pleases, what you never meant" he responds, "Not what he pleases, but what he can." True people will imagine true things, each seeing that which is most appropriately seen in one's present spiritual state and experience.

A successful journey to the Celestial City consists of one's being a true person and devoting oneself to doing true things. This is the only possible course for spiritual success; people must become true beings, face the inescapable demands of spiritual reality, and thus grow into being completely righteous people. This is, of course, the true purpose and end of salvation. God's design and intention is to enable people to become whole and complete in goodness, and His divine grace is present in every aspect of life and experience to help people become what He intends them to be.

LILITH

However, in their perverseness, humans can mysteriously seek to annul the process and sink into ever greater evil. MacDonald depicts his fictional characters as either growing in goodness or deteriorating toward evil; this is essentially true of *Lilith*. In his preface to *Letters from Hell*[2] MacDonald speaks of

> the awful verity, that we make our fate in unmaking ourselves; that men, in defacing the image of God in themselves, construct for themselves a world of horror and dismay; that of the outer darkness our own deeds and character are the informing or inwardly creating cause; that if a man will not have God, he never can be rid of his weary and hateful self.

Viewed in this way, all people are either becoming better or worse spiritually. In *Lilith*, the various characters illustrate both the various impediments to having a successful spiritual journey and the experiences necessary to spiritual triumph.

Vane, the protagonist, is late nineteenth-century man as MacDonald understood him: proud, more scientifically and materially oriented than Anodos, an intellectual to whom spiritual realities are simply "metaphysical" speculations, noumena about which he is curious only as he perceives them affecting the physical world. Such people need to confront the demanding verities of the world of spirit, be made to see how foolish by comparison the self-confident attitudes of scientific rationalism are, and decide either to die into life or face the consequences of selfism. These needs are worked out in Vane's adventures in the "Region of Seven Dimensions," a name that graphically suggests the multifaceted richness of the realm of true spiritual reality.

The central image of this region is Eve's House, to which travelers come to sleep. Sleeping suggests dying into life, that willing forsaking of the self and self-concerns that is requisite to spiritual wholeness. Eve's House is contrasted to the house of Mara, where people who refuse to sleep must face the consequences of their self-nurturing attitudes. Because both Vane and Lilith[3] exhibit obtuse and rebellious attitudes, they proceed to "unmake" themselves. Both must visit Mara. There Vane comes to terms with his own folly; Lilith, who epitomizes the principle of spiritual rebellion and selfishness, must undergo the spiritual horror of seeing the moral grotesque she has made herself to become in contrast to the moral splendor God had originally intended her to be. After this clear-sighted confrontation, she consents to sleep and is taken to Eve's House. Whenever a person chooses to be "rid of his weary and hateful self," that one is freed to sleep, or die into life, allowing God to develop righteousness within.

After Vane refuses to sleep in Eve's House, he enters the Evil Wood, the internal hell he must experience because of his refusal. It is no less real for being a projection of his present spiritual state. The way any person sees the world is shaped by that person's character. "To the pure all things are pure, but to the corrupt and unbelieving nothing is pure; their very minds and consciences are corrupted" (Titus 1:15 RSV; cf. Psalm 18:25–26). MacDonald expresses the thought: "That which is within a man, not that which lies beyond his vision, is the main factor in what is about to befall him" (chapter 16). The terrain of Vane's Evil Wood is formed by his own spiritual perverseness: various monsters rise from the earth to terrorize him. But the moon, which so often in MacDonald's writings symbolizes the governing presence of Divine Providence, oversees his path, making certain each of Vane's experiences is precisely appropriate to his spiritual need.

In the Evil Wood, Vane catches a vision of the "gruesome dance" of damned souls. Their skeletal forms without faces suggest the degree to which their self-centered and evil attitudes have "unmade" their very beings; their spiritual journeys have been disastrous. At one point he sees a multitude in furious battle:

> Wild cries and roars of rage, shock of onset, struggle prolonged, all mingled with words articulate surged in my ears. Curses and credos, snarls and sneers, laughter and mockery, sacred names and howls of hate, came huddling in chaotic interpenetration. . . . The holiest words went with the most hating blow. Lie-distorted truths flew hurtling in the wind of javelins and bones. Every moment some one would turn against his comrades, and fight more wildly than before, The Truth! The Truth! still his cry.

Many religious controversies deteriorate into such fiascos. Foul and contentious attitudes abound, making hell hell. "Our own deeds and character are the informing or inwardly creating cause" of the outer darkness.

Vane also encounters a colony of Little Ones. In contrast to the pervading hatred and contention among the skeletons, they are loving, meek, sensitive, gentle, and fun-loving. They are as well, however, often bungling and ineffectual. MacDonald is making reference to professing religious people whose spirits manifest many spiritually admirable attitudes, but who have not yet come into true spiritual maturity. Lona, who symbolizes Redeeming Love, snatches the Little Ones from Bulika, the worldly city where Lilith reigns, and protects them, but they need to become more spiritually mature. Underneath the ground Vane periodically hears streams of water flowing, an image that suggests the Water of Life. When the Little Ones can avail themselves of it and drink deeply enough, they become ideal beings.

Being a member of this colony does not guarantee one's spiritual journey will be increasingly successful, however. The Little Ones ever face the subtle danger of deteriorating into being Bags, giants whose dominant emotions seem to be anger, greed, and selfishness, and who try to control the Little Ones. They represent a mentality into which professing Christians may fall. Unfortunately, too often such beings are ambitious for positions of importance and leadership, desiring to be lords over people more spiritually meek and modest.

At the close of chapter 41, after Vane has buried Lilith's hand, the final symbol of acquisitiveness, the streams of water, hitherto flowing underground, are released. Like the water of the River of Life that flows from the temple and floods the world in Ezekiel's final vision, these waters begin to fill the land, and MacDonald's vision enters its final phase. It is dynamic, not static; MacDonald is suggesting that this is the farthest reach toward the Celestial City of which the human imagination is capable.

At least three aspects of this final phase deserve especial attention. While Vane is sleeping the glorifying sleep, he faces in a dream all the wrongs he has ever done to others, asks forgiveness, and attempts to right them. All wrongs must be made right; a practical justice must be effected. While Christ effected atonement between humankind and God, humans must effect a practical atonement between each other.

Second, as Vane is troubled with doubt in his dreams, Adam assures him that a certain quality of doubt is inescapable so long as people are imperfect beings: "The hour will come, and that ere long, when being true, thou shalt behold the very truth, and doubt will be for ever dead." So long as the perception of spiritual realities is a matter of faith, an amount of doubt is unavoidable, and must not be a source of guilt.

Third, as the party of awakened people proceed toward the Father, they experience "wondrous" changes both within and without. Vane marvels: "Every growing thing showed me by its shape and colour, its indwelling idea—the informing thought, that is, which was its being." His spirit exults in experiencing in himself and all around him the fruition of the Divine intention, that end toward which all the activity of God throughout time has been steadily moving. "To be aware of a thing, was to know its life at once and mine, to know whence we came, and where we were at home—was to know that we are all what we are, because Another is what he is!"

The fantasy closes with Vane, like Job, being willing patiently to wait for his demise. He does not seek to return to the Region of Seven Dimensions before he is summoned to do so because the wisdom of faith is to wait upon God in confidence, not to satisfy mere curiosity by repeated attempts to return before his time.

The Christian life as MacDonald envisions it, therefore, is a constant process of becoming a whole and righteous person. It begins with that dying into life which is the heart of the new birth, and it proceeds by cooperating with the gracious providence of God that surrounds us, enabling us continually to become more fit to share in His glory. The spiritual process will be consummated for all pilgrims in a final and complete dying into life, or glorification. The end of the journey is the home of the Celestial City, home because God is there. It is with reference to this grand vision of the nature and total purpose of human life that Anodos at the conclusion of *Phantastes* confidently affirms: "Yet I know that good is coming to me—that good is always coming, though few have at all times the simplicity and the courage to belief it. What we call evil, is the only and best shape, which for the person and his condition at the time, could be assumed by the best good."

NOTES

1. These novels have been abridged and "modernized" in paperback form and are available from Bethany House Publishers (Minneapolis) and Scripture Press (Wheaton, Illinois). Because this condensing process has meant the excision of many of the author's rich Christian insights, two companies are now publishing his works in their original forms. Sunrise Books Publishers of Eureka, California, has published many beautifully bound centenary editions of the more popular novels; Johannesen Printing and Publishing of Whitethorn, California, has published the complete works of George MacDonald, in their authentic Victorian binding and format, at economical prices.

2. An anonymous Dutch author first published this book in 1866; it subsequently went through a great many editions. MacDonald, so impressed by its truth, contributed a preface to the 1884 edition. It is no doubt the volume from which C. S. Lewis conceived the notion of writing *Screwtape Letters*.

3. MacDonald gives in chapter 19 his version of the Lilith myth, taken from the Jewish cabala, a myth that was enjoying a certain vogue in the late nineteenth century. As Adam's first wife who rebels against him and normal childbearing, Lilith becomes an apt symbol of selfishness and rebellion to legitimate authority. What she symbolizes may be seen to have apt application to the extreme feminism of our times.

WORKS CITED

The editions of George Macdonald's work used in this essay are listed below, under "Further Reading." For a full account of MacDonald's life and career, consult Rolland Hein, *George MacDonald: Victorian Mythmaker* (Nashville: Star Song, 1993), or, for a summary, Hein's introduction to *The Heart of George MacDonald* (Wheaton, Ill.: Harold Shaw, 1994).

Hein, Rolland. *George MacDonald: Victorian Mythmaker.* Nashville: Star Song, 1993. A critical biography, based on family letters.

MacDonald, George. *At the Back of the North Wind.* 1871. Reprint. Whitethorn, Calif.: Johannesen, 1992.

———. *Alec Forbes of Howglen.* 1865. Reprint. Eureka, Calif.: Sunrise, 1988.

———. *Donal Grant.* 1883. Reprint. Whitethorn, Calif: Johannesen, 1992.

———. *The Heart of George MacDonald.* Edited by Rolland Hein. Wheaton, Ill.: Harold Shaw, 1994. Contains *The Golden Key* (1893) and *The Princess and Curdie* (1883), together with a selection of MacDonald's best writings in various genres.

———. *Lilith A and Lilith 1895: A Duplex.* 1895 (*Lilith A*), 1895 (*Lilith*). Reprint. Whitethorn, Calif.: Johannesen, 1994.

———. *Paul Faber, Surgeon.* 1879. Reprint. Whitethorn, Calif.: Johannesen, 1992..

———. *Phantastes.* 1858. Reprint. Whitethorn, Calif.: Johannesen, 1992.

———. *The Princess and the Goblin.* 1872. Reprint. Whitethorn, Calif.: Johannesen, 1993.

———. *Sir Gibbie.* 1879. Reprint. Whitethorn, Calif.: Johannesen, 1992.

———. *Thomas Wingfold, Curate.* 1896. Reprint. Eureka, Calif.: Sunrise, 1988.

———. *What's Mine's Mine.* 1886. Reprint. Whitethorn, Calif.: Johannesen, 1991.

NINE

LONGING FOR HEAVEN: C. S. LEWIS'S *THE GREAT DIVORCE*

BY WAYNE MARTINDALE

I begin with a confession: I have not always wanted to go to heaven. I can see now that many misconceptions had a grip on my fuzzy, almost unconscious thinking about it. Perhaps my biggest fear, until some time after my undergraduate years, was that heaven would be boring.

I knew I should want to go to heaven, but I didn't. I would have said that I want to go to heaven when I die, but mainly, I just didn't want to go to hell. My problem was a badly warped theology. I knew that in heaven we would worship God forever. But the only model I had for worship was church, and frankly, I wasn't in love with church enough to want it to go on through ages of ages, world without end. My mental image was of Reverend Cant droning on for ever and ever.

Somewhere in the back of my mind, quite unconsciously, heaven was an extended, boring church service like those I had not yet learned to appreciate on earth—with this exception: that you never got to go home to the roast beef dinner. What a way to anticipate my eternal destiny. But then I read *The Great Divorce*. It awakened in me an appetite for something better than roast beef. It aroused a longing to inherit that for which I was created, for that which would fulfill my utmost longings and engender new longings and fulfill those too.

After reading *The Great Divorce*, for the first time in my life, I felt heaven to be both utterly real and utterly desirable. It was a magnificent gift. Small wonder, then, that *The Great Divorce* has always been one of my favorite books, because when I read it, it awakened me to my spiritual anorexia. I was starving for heavenly food and didn't even know I was hungry.

In discussing this book, we'll have to spend a little time in Lewis's imaginary hell, but we'll leave that mildewed place for the fresh outdoor world of heaven before long to look at some of the positive truths that make it so desirable.

First, a disclaimer: Lewis's own. He says in the Preface that he is not attempting to describe either hell or heaven as he thinks it literally appears as landscape. His real concerns are to show that heaven is more real than any present physical reality and is the fulfillment of God's desires for us, and that hell is by comparison "so nearly nothing." He is also concerned to show that people choose their own eternal destiny by turning them-selves—with the Devil's help or Christ's—into souls fit for hell or souls fit for heaven.

Throughout his works, Lewis's most persistent theme is our desire for heaven. Lacking a word to adequately describe this inmost hunger, he borrows one from Wordsworth and Coleridge: The word is *joy*. It is a problematical term in that its usual meaning is happiness, satisfaction, and fulfillment, whereas Lewis's special use is nearly the opposite: It is the absence of satisfaction and fulfillment. He defines joy as a "stab of desire" for something never satisfied on earth. When all of our natural desires have been fulfilled, "we remain conscious of a desire which no natural happiness will satisfy" ("Weight" 8). For this reason, it is a major pointer to heaven and was key in Lewis's own conversion (see Lewis's *Surprised by Joy*).

Lewis believed that every desire is at its root a desire for heaven. Solomon agrees, noting that God has put eternity in our hearts (Ecclesi-astes 3:11). Augustine put it this way: "Our heart is restless, until it repose in thee." We are all pilgrims in search of the Celestial City: some lost and looking for "joy" in all the wrong places, some saved with eyes fixed on the heavenly prize, some sidetracked on dead-end streets and byways—but all longing for heaven, whether we know it or not. Nearly all of Lewis's works (seventy-two in the Lowenberg bibliography) have the aim of arousing this desire for heaven or showing us how to live in proper anticipation of our true home.

Heaven is more sharply defined and more keenly desired when contrasted with hell. So Lewis's story, like Dantes', opens in hell. Also like Dante, Lewis gives his own name to the character who journeys from hell to heaven and narrates the story. And as Dante has his mentor Virgil for a guide, so Lewis has his mentor as guide. Lewis had his desires for heaven aroused at the age of sixteen when he read George MacDonald's *Phantastes*, so exactly halfway through *The Great Divorce*, on the outskirts of heaven, the narrator Lewis meets George MacDonald, who becomes his teacher.

In Lewis's story, all who are in hell can take a bus to heaven, if they wish, though few even wish it. Does Lewis believe that souls in hell actually have a "second chance"? Absolutely not. He says in the Preface that he chose *The Great Divorce* as the title to deliberately contradict William Blake's notion expressed in the title "The Marriage of Heaven and Hell," a satiric reworking of Milton, which claims that "the road of excess leads to the palace of wisdom" (Keynes xviii), and that opposites must marry before progress is possible. As Lewis says, reality presents us with an "'either-or.' If we insist on keeping hell (or even earth) we shall not see heaven: if we accept heaven we shall not be able to retain even the smallest and most intimate souvenirs of hell" (6). Lewis deliberately casts the whole story as a dream-vision (as we learn at the end) to emphasize the fictional nature of the story: and anything can happen in dreams.

Why, then, does Lewis allow the "hellians" to journey to heaven and stay if they want? Simply to stress (1) that we choose our eternal destinies and (2) that by our life choices we turn ourselves into beings suited for one or the other. By presenting his characters at the entrance to heaven, Lewis can show at once both the process that damns and the result. We hear the hellians' reasons for rejecting heaven, and as they leave for the "grey town" (hell), we instantly see the consequence. Tellingly, those from hell usually fail to even see the beauties of heaven and most hasten back to hell. As Lewis said in *The Problem of Pain*:

We are afraid that heaven is a bribe, and that if we make it our goal we shall no longer be disinterested. It is not so. Heaven offers nothing that a mercenary soul can desire. It is safe to tell the pure in heart that they shall see God, for only the pure in heart want to. (145)

In illustration of this point, the very first Ghost from the grey town to be mentioned (besides the narrator) doesn't last even a minute in heaven. "'I don't like it! I don't like it,' screamed a voice, 'It gives me the pip!'" (28). With that she ran to the bus and never returned.

When the narrator Lewis asks his teacher if everyone has a chance to get on the bus, MacDonald replies with these soaring words:

Everyone who wishes it does. Never fear. There are only two kinds of people in the end: those who say to God, "*Thy* will be done," and those to whom God says, in the end, "*Thy* will be done." All that are in Hell, choose it. Without that self-choice there could be no Hell. No soul that seriously and constantly desires joy will ever miss it. Those who seek find. To those who knock it is opened. (72–73)

The theme of choice and our responsibility to choose not only permeates *The Great Divorce*, but is found throughout Lewis's works. Here's another example from *The Problem of Pain:*

In the long run the answer to all those who object to the doctrine of hell is itself a question: "What are you asking God to do?" To wipe out their past sins and, at all costs, to give them a fresh start, smoothing every difficulty and offering every miraculous help? But He has done so, on Calvary. To forgive them? They will not be forgiven. To leave them alone? Alas, I am afraid that is what He does. (128)

DESCENT INTO HELL

The technique of using contrasts, discussed in Ryken's chapter on methodology, is central to Lewis's success in portraying heaven as desirable and hell as repulsive. From the beginning, even before we learn that the story has opened in hell, we find the place to be uncomfortable, dreary, drab, deserted, and literally hollow since it is a largely unoccupied shell. The people we encounter are peevish, self-centered, grasping, and unpleasant.

In *The Great Divorce*, we never enter deep hell or deep heaven: We are only on the outskirts of each. Lewis's opening vision of hell is people standing in line, waiting for a bus. How prophetic for our culture. What two things can you think of that Westerners, especially Americans, hate more than doing without their cars and standing in line? To a fast food, drive-thru culture like ours, lines are hell. On top of that, hell in *The Great Divorce* is a foggy, drippy, deserted, twilight place. It is, in other words, an endless English winter; and to the English, who love to garden and walk, that is hell.

To the narrator's surprise, hell is deserted. It's deserted because in hell you can have anything you want by just wishing for it. Of course, the whole point of hell is that you don't wish for the right things. People there are always getting into arguments with the folks next door and wishing new houses into existence farther away from their nettlesome neighbors so that hell is ever expanding. Napoleon is the nearest of the old rouges of history, and it took a visiting party fifteen thousand years to get to his place, only to discover him pacing back and forth. They watched him for a year, and all he ever did was pace and mutter, "It was Soult's fault. It was Ney's fault. It was Josephine's fault," and so on, endlessly.

We may be tempted to think that hell will be an entertaining place because it will have so many colorful people—a bully social club. It's the glimmer of fool's gold. Like Napoleon, all in hell have become the sin they have chosen, unillumined by the common grace of God scattered broadcast upon the earth. Nothing is more boring than the tawdry and unrelieved self. What a deception I had been under! I was afraid of heaven because I thought it would be boring, when all along it was hell I should have feared. In Lewis's *Great Divorce*, I saw that hell is a boring place peopled with bores. It should not surprise us that there are no pleasures in hell. In *The Screwtape Letters*, Lewis has the senior devil Screwtape lament while cautioning the junior tempter Wormwood:

> Never forget that when we are dealing with any pleasure in its healthy and normal and satisfying form, we are, in a sense, on the Enemy's ground. I know we have won many a soul through pleasure. All the same, it is His invention, not ours. He made the pleasures: all our research so far has not enabled us to produce one. All we can do is to encourage the humans to take the pleasures which our Enemy has produced, at times, or in ways, or in degrees, which He has forbidden. Hence we always try to work away from the natural condition of any pleasure to that in which it is least natural, least

redolent of its Maker, and least pleasurable. An ever increasing craving for an ever diminishing pleasure is the formula. (Letter IX)

Hell is the absence of God, and God is the author of all the pleasures, as Augustine, Dante, Milton, MacDonald, and Lewis illustrate at length in the works covered by this book. Heaven is that place where all that is and all that happens issues out of God's creative genius. In that sense, it's like the beauties of earth, except that here even nature groans, waiting for its deliverance from the curse of sin. If we like the good things of earth, we will love heaven. God through Christ invented all the earthly pleasures, and He is the same one now preparing a place for us and will come again to receive us to Himself. The psalmist says: "In thy presence is fulness of joy; at thy right hand there are pleasures for evermore" (Psalm 16:11 KJV).

ASCENT INTO HEAVEN

Lewis has another good reason for allowing the trip from hell to heaven: to provide for multiple contrasts as a way of highlighting both hellish and heavenly qualities, contrasts between physical things, such as landscapes and bodies, and contrasts in the character of these people.

Upon arriving at heaven, the first thing the narrator notices is its expansiveness. Though hell seemed expansive from within, by contrast to heaven, it is claustrophobic. Heaven "made the Solar System itself an indoor affair" (27). We later learn that the hellians, though it seemed to them a long journey up the side of a cliff, emerged in heaven from a minuscule crack in the soil between two blades of grass. If a butterfly of heaven were to swallow all of hell, the teacher, MacDonald, tells the narrator, it would make no more difference than swallowing a single atom (122–23). How real is heaven, how much more substantial? Hell could not contain the minutest part of it.

After the landscape, the next thing the narrator notices is the bodies of the hellians. They appear as ghosts, as dirty stains on the air. Because people in hell are really remains of their human selves with their potential shriveled by sin, when they are expanded to the size of a normal person in heaven, they are so thin and unsubstantial that they look like ghosts. This is a very effective technique for showing that heaven is ultimate reality and hell so nearly nothing.

But the most telling contrast comes in the character of the people. The diabolical and warped are met by the holy and whole. Those from heaven are fulfilled, content, overflowing with love and the reflected glory of Christ that makes them luminous. The Ghosts have all come to heaven for some bogus and selfish reason. The Solid People, as those from heaven are called, have all made great sacrifices to come long distances from deep heaven to the outskirts in hopes of winning some of the Ghosts to heaven.

The longest journey, however, is made by Christ Himself. We know from some key, though subtle, clues that the bus driver who brings the Ghosts to heaven is representative of Christ. First, the narrator's teacher, MacDonald, says that only the greatest can become small enough to fit into hell. Second, the driver is described as being "full of light." Third, He is rejected by those He came to save: "God! I'd like to give him one in the ear-'ole," snarls one of the Ghosts. The narrator responds: "I could see nothing in the countenance of the Driver to justify all this, unless it were that he had a look of authority and seemed intent on carrying out his job" (14). This episode is a literal enactment of the Apostles' Creed: "He descended into hell."

What follows upon their arrival in heaven is a series of loosely organized encounters between the Ghosts and appropriate heavenly counterparts. As with its cousin, *The Screwtape Letters*, the design is episodic: There isn't much plot. Although we come to identify with the narrator and his final fate, the interest is not mainly in the resolution of a central conflict or the development of a single character. Rather, our interest is in what sort of persons will take the stage next, what has kept them from heaven, and what their response will be to the invitation to enter all joy. In the process, we get a short course on human nature and the psychology of sin.

Also like *The Screwtape Letters*, in *The Great Divorce* Lewis blends elements of earth with his vision of hell. In the latter book, he blends elements of earth with heaven too. This not only makes hell and heaven more understandable because of the familiar earthly elements, but it makes us grasp the truth that "there is no neutral ground in the universe: every square inch, every split second, is claimed by God and counter claimed Satan" in a battle for our souls ("Culture" 33). It also points up the further truth that we bring into our earthly experience intimations of either heaven or hell by our choices. We are becoming every moment souls suited for one or the other.

You will have met people who are so full of the spirit of Christ that any destiny other than heaven is unthinkable. These people also have many of the joys that will characterize heaven, even in the midst of earthly pain. You will also have met people who hate goodness: who prefer evil companions and evil acts, though it makes them wretched and miserable. When they do encounter good persons, they condemn them, perverting their reason by rationalizing evil and finding ways to blame the good or God or religion for their problems and the problems of the world. They already hate goodness because it implicitly condemns the evil they have chosen. They wouldn't like heaven if they could have it. They are, in a sense, already in hell, preferring darkness to light. This we see in each of the Ghosts that returns to hell.

On the book's design, Evan Gibson notes, the Ghosts and the people from heaven who meet them are presented in three divisions: five in the first half, five in the last half, and a group in the middle getting short treatment, all the hellians having in common a foolish desire to criticize heaven. Some come all the way from hell just to spit at heaven in spite (116). The first five Ghosts are all inwardly focused. Their besetting sins are: "their inflated inner-image, their intellectual dishonesty, their materialism, their cynicism, their false shame" (Gibson 121). The five in the second half are also selfish, but their sin involves the desire to control others. Except for the first one, an artist, all in this last group exhibit some kind of perverted family relationship.

As with *The Screwtape Letters*, we learn by negative example how not to behave and by inference how we should behave. It is a series of lessons in kingdom values, like the parables of Jesus. From the Theological Ghost, we learn that we can slip from a desire to know God and a love of God to a desire to know about God and a love of mere academic, theological pursuit. The Theological Ghost would rather return to hell where he can dispute about Christ than enter heaven and know Him.

Similarly, the Painter Ghost has slipped from loving light and truth to loving the medium to loving his own opinions of truth to loving his reputation. He learns from a heavenly counterpart that no one is much interested in his work now that he has been dead a while. He instantly abandons heaven in a vain attempt to restore his now discredited reputation and resurrect his school of painting. Journals, lectures, manifestos, publicity—these fill his mind as he abandons Truth and ultimately his true self for pretensions.

We also meet a mother who is possessive of her son and a wife whose earthly life was devoted to remaking her husband in her own image. Both would rather see their family members in hell for the chance of controlling them than find true love in heaven, love that cares about the real good of another. In the process of grasping, like all the hellians, they pervert their own personalities and become the sin they choose. Though on the brink of heaven, all the Ghosts from hell could say with Milton's Satan:

> The mind is its own place, and in itself
> Can make a Heaven of Hell, a Hell of Heaven.
> (*Paradise Lost* 1.254–55)
> Which way I fly is Hell; myself am Hell.
> (*Paradise Lost* 4.75)

The Great Divorce shows us a parallel truth, one preeminently displayed in Dante's vision: that neither the punishment of hell nor the reward of heaven is arbitrary. Lewis's heavenly guide, MacDonald, explains this in the case of the Grumbling Ghost:

> The whole difficulty of understanding Hell is that the thing to be understood is so nearly Nothing. But ye'll have had experiences . . . it begins with a grumbling mood, and yourself still distinct from it: perhaps criticising it. And yourself, in a dark hour, may will that mood, embrace it. Ye can repent and come out of it again. But there may come a day when you can do that no longer. Then there will be not you left to criticise the mood, nor even to enjoy it, but just the grumble itself going on forever like a machine. (75)

One of the central truths the book teaches is that heaven is the fulfillment of human potential, hell the drying up of human potential. "To enter heaven is to become more human than you ever succeeded in being in earth; to enter hell, is to be banished from humanity. What is cast (or casts itself) into hell is not a man: it is 'remains'" (*Pain* 125). Hell strips away distinctions, and unrelieved sin is shown to be boring. On the other hand, in heaven we blossom into fully differentiated personalities.

> If He had no use for all these differences, I do not see why He should have created more souls than one. Be sure that the ins and outs of your individuality are no mystery to Him; and one day they will no longer be a mystery to you. . . . All that you are, sins apart, is destined, if you will let God have

His good way, to utter satisfaction. . . . Your place in heaven will seem to be made for you and you alone, because you were made for it. (*Pain* 147–48)

Having seen the long parade of Ghosts who come to the outskirts of heaven only to return to hell for the same reason they went there in the first place, the narrator naturally inquires of his guide whether any actually accept the invitation to enter heaven. There are allusions by MacDonald to many who make it in, but we only see one actually making the passage. This is the case of a man whose besetting sin is lust, symbolized by a red lizard who sits on his shoulder, reminding him that his very identity is wrapped up in his lust and that life would be insipid without the flame of desire. An angel meets the Lustful Ghost and implores him for permission to kill the lizard. Through many struggles and though fearful that it may mean his death, he gives permission. Wondrously, the lizard is transformed into a white stallion, which the now Solid Man rides joyously into heaven.

The point is not that people once in hell can go to heaven or that sin can progress to goodness: Lewis explicitly denies both, as we have seen. The point is (1) that we must die to self to live and (2) that all desires, however masked, are ultimately for heaven. When we give our desires to God, the Author of all the pleasures, He fulfills the desires. The very thing which when grasped would drag us to hell and pervert our personalities, when given to God is not only fulfilled but becomes a means of grace. God created all things good. Sin is not self-existent; it is a perversion of good.

A word on the Solid People: none in the book who come from deep heaven to meet the Ghosts are "great" in an earthly sense. The only one besides Lewis with a popular earthly reputation is his guide, MacDonald. The others are all ordinary people with sins running the gambut from pride in one's own talent to apostasy to murder. The main difference is that the Solid People all recognized their need of God and repented— turned from their sin and received the gift of a new heart (new motives) and eternal life. None suffers the illusion that he or she deserves heaven. It is a completely undeserved gift. The Solid People urge each of the Ghosts to receive the gift and "enter into joy." Pride keeps them out. All try to justify their sin. One of the impressions we are left with is how easy heaven is to gain and how easy it is to lose.

Lewis's journey motif, with its setting in hell and heaven, makes possible some very effective puns that throw common phrases into a new light. The first Ghost into heaven to get extended treatment is simply called "The Big Man" in hell and "The Big Ghost" in heaven. He is met from heaven by Len, a man who had worked for him and who had murdered a mutual acquaintance named Jack. Upon seeing that Len was a Solid Person and robed in heavenly splendor, the first words out of the Big Ghost's mouth are, "Well, I'm damned" (32). He spoke as he always had on earth, blaspheming to show his surprise, but now it is literally true, which one look at the solid Len confirms by contrast with his ghostly self.

Len explains that the burden of seeing himself as a murderer had driven him to Christ. The Big Ghost merely persists in claiming the unfairness of it all, he having been a decent chap, and he keeps demanding "his rights." Ironically, the Big Ghost and all in hell have precisely that: their rights. All sin; all deserve hell. As Len urges him to forget about himself and his rights, the Ghost, saying more than he knows, says, "'I'm not asking for anybody's bleeding charity'" (34). In Britain, "bleeding" in this usage is a profane oath referring to Christ's blood, which is literally his only hope of heaven. Len replies, "'Then do. At once. Ask for the Bleeding Charity. Everything is here for the asking and nothing can be bought'" (34).

Language usage has come full circle from concrete heavenly truth to profane abstraction back to literal heavenly truth. We laugh, we see with new insight, we blush, and, one hopes, we repent. Meanwhile, The Big Ghost, stubborn as a mule about accepting any heaven that admits murderers like Len, concludes, "'I'd rather be damned than go along with you. I came here to get my rights, see? Not to go snivelling along on charity tied onto your apron-strings. If they're too fine to have me without you, I'll go home'" (36). So he goes "home" to hell.

The last paired Ghost and Solid Person are treated at the greatest length and deserve special attention. Here, using the technique of analogy (using the earthly to describe the heavenly), we have Lewis's fullest description of a Solid Person. Throughout the book, Lewis has used the technique of distancing. Scripture says, "No eye has seen, nor ear heard, nor the human heart conceived, what God has prepared for those who love him" (1 Corinthians 2:9 NRSV). Since heaven is beyond our experience or even our imagining, Lewis avoids error and enhances our anticipation of it by never giving us a glimpse of "deep heaven" or even "deep hell." Throughout the narrative, we are always in the in-between time before night falls in hell or the day dawns in heaven. Geographically, we are also never allowed into hell or heaven proper; we are always on the outskirts. Yet what we see of the fringes is both unspeakably horrific and unspeakably enchanting by comparison to earth. But even here on the outskirts, we see enough to make our blood run fast.

In the last pairing, a self-pitying Ghost named Frank appears as a Dwarf leading by a chain a projection of himself called a Tragedian. He is met by Sarah Smith of Golders Green, who was his wife on earth. Frank's interest in making the pilgrimage from hell is not in gaining heaven; it is for gaining pity for his condition, thereby holding the joy of heaven hostage. In this Lewis answers the age-old question of how there could be joy in heaven when even one soul suffers the torments of everlasting hell. Pity cannot hold love hostage. MacDonald, the narrator's guide, explains to him that heaven will not make a dunghill of "the world's garden for the sake of some who cannot abide the smell of roses" (121). In the end, the Dwarf Frank chooses his self-pity over heaven and shrinks until nothing is left but the projection of his sin, the Tragedian, which vanishes back to the constriction that is hell.

Sarah is not brokenhearted; it is not possible in the presence of Him who is true love and joy. She is joined by angels who sing a psalm of her overcoming joy and protection by God. She appears by earthly standards to be a goddess. Indeed, she is a "Great One" in heaven, though on earth she was the lady next door. She is reaping the rewards of nameless acts of love that characterized every contact with every person and all creation. This love extended even to the animals. Now, in heaven, these very animals make up a part of her sizable entourage, which also included gigantic emerald angels scattering flowers, followed by numerous boys and girls, and musicians. Of the indescribably beautiful music, the narrator can only say that no one who "read that score would ever grow sick or old" (107). "Dancing light" shined from the entourage. All was in honor of Sarah Smith, who was so gloriously ordinary on earth. And to this the Self-Pitying ghost and all from hell were invited. We wonder at the depth of pride and perversion that would enable so many, both in the book and in our own experience, to thumb their noses at the sublime largesse of God.

So often in Lewis, what we find illustrated in the fiction, we find explained in the nonfiction. The nonfiction counterpart to this portrait of Sarah Smith is the vaulting passage toward the end of Lewis's great sermon, "The Weight of Glory":

> It may be possible for each to think too much of his own potential glory hereafter; it is hardly possible for him to think too often or too deeply about that of his neighbour. The load, or weight, or burden of my neighbour's glory should be laid on my back, a load so heavy that only humility can carry it, and the backs of the proud will be broken. It is a serious thing to live in a society of possible gods and goddesses, to remember that the dullest and most uninteresting person you can talk to may one day be a creature which, if you saw it now, you would be strongly tempted to worship, or else a horror and a corruption such as you now meet, if at all, only in a nightmare. All day long we are, in some degree, helping each other to one or the other of these destinations. It is in the light of these overwhelming possibilities, it is with the awe and the circumspection proper to them, that we should conduct all our dealings with one another, all friendships, all loves, all play, all politics. There are no *ordinary* people. You have never talked to a mere mortal. (18–19)

The Great Divorce ends with dizzying reflections on time and eternity, predestination and free will. Lewis deftly shows that all attempts to solve this ancient paradox fail if they are posed from within time. God, being outside of time, sees all in an ever-present now, so from His point of view, all is known and done, even what is yet in the future for us. But from our point of view within time, choices are still before us.

Even now, in what may be my twentieth reading of *The Great Divorce*, the concluding pages move me to tears for people without the hope of the Celestial City and my own destiny were it not for "Bleeding Charity." Throughout the book, it has been perpetual evening twilight in the Grey Town of hell and perpetual pre-sunrise dawn in the hinterlands of heaven where the meetings take place. Now at the end, as Lewis the pilgrim narrator looks into the face of his teacher, George MacDonald, and with the east at his back, the promised sunrise breaks. It will mean eternal day for heaven and a darkening to eternal night for hell. The sunlight falls in solid blocks upon the narrator's insubstantial body, and he is stricken with terror, for he has come to these precincts of heaven as a Ghost from hell: "'The morning! The morning!' I cried, 'I am caught by the morning and I am a ghost'" (128). In the moment he is seized by the terror of damnation, the narrator awakens from his dream, clutching at a tablecloth and pulling down on his head, not blocks of light, but books. With sweet relief, we realize that he and we are still pilgrims and the Celestial City is still before us. There is yet time to choose and to guide the choice of others.

WORKS CITED

Blake, William. *The Marriage of Heaven and Hell*. Edited by Geoffrey Keynes. New York: Oxford Univ. Press, 1975.

Gibson, Evan K. *C. S. Lewis, Spinner of Tales: A Guide to His Fiction*. Grand Rapids: Eerdmans, 1980.

Lewis, C. S. "Christianity and Culture." In *Christian Reflections*. Grand Rapids: Eerdmans, 1967.

————. *The Great Divorce*. New York: Macmillan, 1946.

————. *The Problem of Pain*. New York: Macmillan, 1962.

————. *The Screwtape Letters*. New York: Macmillan, 1962.

————. *Surprised by Joy*. New York: Harcourt, Brace & World, 1955.

————. "The Weight of Glory." In *The Weight of Glory and Other Addresses*. Revised. New York: Macmillan, 1980.

Milton, John. *The Complete Poems and Major Prose*. Edited by Merritt Hughes. New York: Odyssey, 1957.

FURTHER READING

Macmillan publishes an inexpensive paperback edition of *The Great Divorce* (New York, 1946). You may want to consider Macmillan's boxed set of six paperbacks, called *Six by Lewis*, which includes *The Great Divorce*, *The Screwtape Letters*, *Mere Christianity*, *The Problem of Pain*, *The Abolition of Man*, and *Miracles*.

See also Lewis's *Perelandra* (his personal favorite; Macmillan, 1987). Though it is closer to an imagined pre-fallen earth, it is also evocative of heaven and provokes a longing for it in the reader. Other such glimpses into heaven are scattered throughout the Narnia books, the conclusion of *The Last Battle* being my personal favorite. For an allegorical search for heaven, see *The Pilgrim's Regress*, the first book Lewis wrote after becoming a Christian at age thirty-three.

There are no entire books on *The Great Divorce*, but many book-length treatments of Lewis's work have useful short summaries or commentaries on it. The best longer treatments are the following:

C. N. Manlove is one of the few British scholars to write on Lewis but is one of the best. See his *C. S. Lewis: His Literary Achievement* (London: Macmillan, 1987).

Thomas Howard is always interesting and insightful. His style is the most engaging of those listed. See *The Achievement of C. S. Lewis: A Reading of His Fiction* (Wheaton, Ill.: Harold Shaw, 1980). Ignatius Press reissued the volume in 1990 under the title *C. S. Lewis: Man of Letters: A Reading of His Fiction*.

For a good episode-by-episode treatment of the meetings in heaven, see Evan K. Gibson, *C. S. Lewis, Spinner of Tales: A Guide to His Fiction* (Grand Rapids: Eerdmans, 1980).

Leanne Payne has a short but worthwhile treatment of *The Great Divorce* in the Appendix to her *Real Presence: The Christian Worldview of C. S. Lewis as Incarnational Reality* (Wheaton, Ill.: Crossway, 1980; revised 1988; reissued by Baker, 1995).